THE RONIN

THE
RONIN

A Novel Based on a Zen Myth

WILLIAM DALE JENNINGS

Tony:
this is one of my
very favorite books.
Good luck at college!

John

7/30/06

TUTTLE PUBLISHING
Boston • Rutland, VT • Tokyo

This edition published in 2001 by Tuttle Publishing, an imprint of Periplus Editions (HK) Ltd., with editorial offices at 153 Milk Street, Boston, Massachusetts 02109. First published by Charles E. Tuttle Publishing Co., Inc. in 1968.

Library of Congress Catalog Card Number: 68-25890

ISBN: 0-8048-3414-8

Distributed by:

North America
Tuttle Publishing
364 Innovation Drive
North Clarendon, VT 05759-9436
Tel: (802) 773-8930
Fax: (802) 773-6993
Email: info@tuttlepublishing.com
Web site: www.tuttlepublishing.com

Asia Pacific
Berkeley Books Pte. Ltd.
130 Joo Seng Road
#06-01/03 Olivine Building
Singapore 368357
Tel: (65) 6280-3320
Fax: (65) 6280-6290
Email: inquiries@periplus.com.sg
Web site: www.periplus.com

Japan
Tuttle Publishing
Yaekari Building, 3rd Floor
5-4-12 Ōsaki, Shinagawa-ku, Tokyo
Japan 141-0032
Tel: (03) 5437-0171
Fax: (03) 5437-0755
Email: tuttle-sales@gol.com

Indonesia
PT Java Books Indonesia
JI. Kelapa Gading Kirana
Blok A14 No. 17
Jakarta 14240 Indonesia
Tel: (62-21) 451-5351
Fax: (62-21) 453-4987
Email: cs@javabooks.co.id

08 07 06 05 04   9 8 7 6 5 4
Printed in the United States of America

This, of course, is dedicated to

WARD

TABLE OF CONTENTS

I	*A great rustling behind him.* . . .	13
II	*Watching from the shadows.* . . .	19
III	*The honore of bchosening.* . . .	25
IV	*The gifts of hate.* . . .	32
V	*A small extravagance.* . . .	38
VI	*The inevitable flaw.* . . .	44
VII	*Patterns on the pond.* . . .	47
VIII	*Softly, do not wake the child.* . . .	52
IX	*These splendid sins.* . . .	57
X	*The white fist of fortune.* . . .	63
XI	*A delicious tilt of her head.* . . .	69
XII	*The wave-tossed man.* . . .	77
XIII	*Instructions to a dead samurai.* . . .	81
XIV	*Rage and adoration.* . . .	88
XV	*Matriculation.* . . .	93
XVI	*The jackass who is my teacher.* . . .	98
XVII	*Four feet of bamboo.* . . .	103

XVIII *The interruption. . . .*   109
  XIX *The journey through Hell with a torch* 116
   XX *The visiting hour for prisoners. . . .*   122
  XXI *Chaos and the painted tree. . . .*   127
 XXII *A navel for the Gut of Wrath. . . .*   132
XXIII *One more holy showman. . . .*   138
 XXIV *Monster's heir. . . .*   141
  XXV *Another young man dies. . . .*   144
 XXVI *A black lacquer box. . . .*   151
XXVII *And become what I am. . . .*   155

I first heard this story from Nyogen Senzaki in his noisy little duplex on the east side of Los Angeles where incense and tiny bells mingled with fried onions and the shouts of neighbor children. After he'd gone, I found it again among his hundred and one ancient stories in *Zen Flesh, Zen Bones*. Because it seems to be one of those legends containing everything that it is necessary to know, I have played at expanding it a little but, of course, have added nothing.

When Heaven is about to confer
A great office upon a man,
It first exercises his mind with suffering,
And his sinews and bones with toil;
It exposes him to poverty
And confounds all his undertakings.
Then it is seen if he is ready.

—Mōshi

A great rustling behind him. . . .

The muscles of his naked calves bulged below his worn and dirty kimono. The dark cloth flapped behind him as he strode with chest out and sword over one shoulder. The top-knot stood high on the back of his head as a badge and a warning. Everything about him declared: *I have earned this.*

Approaching the village, his stride slowed to caution. There was something different here. Delapidated like most villages in the time of the Gempei, it lacked the terrible melancholy of the thousand others he'd passed through. Here, there was a certain waiting. Something momentous was going to happen in this village.

The young Ronin took the sword from his shoulder and slid it under the *obi* bound low around his waist. The street had been fairly busy for a village this small. At his gesture, the drab little 浪

人

peasants began to fade away like ink in stirred water.

In a moment they'd be closing the *amado* and barring their doors from the inside. He went quickly into the rice shop and sat straight at the table for several moments. Then he ruined the facsimile of dignity by hitting the boards with his palm and shouting, *"Gohan!"*

The rice that the old shopkeeper put before him was steaming—and peculiarly delicious. He gorged the first bowl and savored the second. The shopkeeper's kindly smile spoiled the whole meal for him, though. In view of what must happen when it was over, he would have much preferred the usual sullenness.

At last the hulking young warrior finished, put the *hashi* across the empty bowl and sat sucking bits of rice from his teeth. That done, he laid a big hand on either side of the bowl, took a deep breath and said to the empty room, "No money." His voice was very deep. The answer came from behind him wearily, "I know, I know." He looked over his shoulder: "Go on. Cry. Complain. Call me names. I won't hurt you. The rice was good."

There was a time of silence in the little shop, then the voice behind him said simply, "Coward."

The table went over. The bowl and *hashi* flew. The big man was standing with long sword drawn and rage in his eyes. There was no change in the shopkeeper. He seemed to have resigned himself to this moment long, long ago. He asked, "To eat without first asking, *is* the coward's way, isn't it?" He smiled: "Were you afraid I'd refuse you?"

The sword blurred. Two of the man's fingers pattered on the floor. As if without sensation, he said, "We thought you might be different. Our scout way down the road was sure you were. But it is difficult to see this close what he saw at a distance. We wanted to buy protection. . . ." The blood had begun dripping swiftly, but he continued to smile: "Yes, protection from such as you." He looked wistfully down at the sad little things on the floor: "But two fingers out of ten are a small cost for not making so grand a mistake."

The barbaric young man grunted, "Then let's raise the price." When the blur had ceased, the shopkeeper's hand thudded softly to the floor. He looked at it then sat down slowly in his own blood to wait for death.

The Ronin said, "Yes, you sit there for a while and figure out who's afraid now." The fading figure on the floor looked at the big man from foot to head and said, "To fear is not to be a coward. I've been told that the samurai who has never died is apt to run and hide in decisive moments."

The Ronin didn't really hear him until much later. Right now faces were staring in at the window. He shouted at them angrily, "Oh, don't look so pious and appalled! All of you wish you were man enough to make your own laws as I do. You're only

浪
人
15

honest because you have to be!" Then he wiped his sword clean with a white square of paper.

The young Ronin strode grandly out into the middle of the road. Completely alone, he stood with legs spread and parted his kimono below the *obi* knot. He slid a big hand into the front of his pouch, pulled out a surprise of size and held the kimono open with both hands as a great golden arc glittered in the sun and splattered his bare ankles.

He looked around him like an angry eagle. The fact that he saw no one was satisfactory proof that he was the center of all attention. His anger lessened with the arc and he again felt the difference of the village. It wasn't sad and it *should* have been. He felt the uneasiness of one sensing ambush.

The door of the rice shop slid open, an old monk came out and walked directly toward him. He was small as a boy and amazingly wrinkled. He stopped before the towering young man and said, "You're under arrest. Give me your sword."

The Ronin could only laugh; he continued laughing as he shook off the last drops. He grinned down at the little old man: "Pretty damned big, huh?" The monk looked at it a little sadly: "Perhaps, but a samurai is not his sword."

For the second time that day, deep anger took him. This was far more than a personal insult. The very core of *Bushido* declared that a swordsman *is* his sword. He growled by rote, "It is my living soul." The tiny man held out his hand, "Give it to me. I'll take your soul." The young warrior's eyes were midnight: "Go away quickly, little man. What is a swordsman without his sword?"

The answer came promptly and simply: "A man."

With one great circular gesture, the Ronin drew his sword and halved the old man. With blade frozen at the end of the arc, he stood for the sublime moment that a man waits for his enemy to fall. In it he was shocked to hear that voice say, *"You are still under arrest."* Then the little figure toppled and seemed to explode in blood.

The young warrior was still shaking with anger as he wiped his blade clean with another square of white paper. He tossed it upon the yet moving body that lay in a lazy cloud of dust, slid the sword into its scabbard, cutting edge up, and started to leave the village. A few yards later, he stopped, thrust back his hips and crammed himself back into the pouch. As he did so, a great rustling rose behind him.

Without looking back, he knew they were rushing to their old monk. He'd probably been the pride of the village. There was always a patriarch. But he'd be replaced soon enough by anyone with the proper load of years and wrinkles to hide his confusion. The Ronin grunted as he remembered the little man holding out his hand and saying, "Give me your sword." How painfully sad to behold a man who is both brave and weak!

He had just reached the crossroad a few *ri* from

浪
人

the village when he heard the running feet. It was a young boy. He stopped a safe distance away and held out a piece of white paper folded in the shape of an *L*. The Ronin made him bring it within reaching distance and stand close as he unfolded the paper. The boy stared at the sword-handle. The big man smiled, "Oho, I can see you want to grow up to be a samurai, too, huh?"

The boy looked up at him in grave disapproval and said, "Oh, no." Then he turned and walked back down the road into the infinity from which he'd come.

The calligraphy was expert: *"The writer of this note wishes to deliver an urgent message to you. It is of the greatest importance that you be at this crossroad at the Hour of the Ram . . . one year from today."*

He read the words a second time and then a third. Giving up, he crumpled the page angrily in a big fist and tossed it away from him. Looking back down the road, he shouted, "Your whole damned village is bewitched! First, I'm called a coward by a shopkeeper, then an old monk tries to arrest me. Now a boy says no to the glory of steel, and someone invites me to come back here for a meeting so urgent it can wait a year! Bewitched, bewitched!"

He started on his way then stopped again and shouted back: *"This place is cursed! Nothing in all Heaven or Hell could make me come back here again!"* The young Ronin whirled and strode quickly out onto the silent plain.

Watching from the shadows. . . .

The next village north called itself *Hachiman's Hunger* in much the same way that, eight centuries later, another country would remember the places where its first president rested for the night. In turn, its neighbor on the north was named *Tenth Verse Ox* or, to stretch it for the wide screen, *The Ox of the Tenth Verse,* a name of fabulous meaning.

Because the third neighbor north was unusually distant and few had ever been there, the Ox people often had to take a breath before recalling its name. For this reason, it came to be known as *The Place of the Forgotten Name* even to those who lived there. It was in this third village that there lived three strong young boys who spent all the hours of their days dashing headlong toward manhood as if it really existed. They were the closest of friends, and all shared the same dream. At the age of eleven, they decided to become samurai, or professional swordsmen, in the train of some mighty *daimyo*. However 浪人

childish the ambition, it was the correct age to start learning.

Of course, they never once considered the possibility that they might all three live out their brief lives as mere ronin or unemployed samurai wanderers of which there were thousands rejected by both *Gen* and *Hei*. Nor did it occur to them that their parents might begrudge this time stolen from the never-finished work in the fields, nor that the local master swordsman (retired) might refuse to accept them as students. He was a proud man and a genius by implication: few swordsmen of that time retired in the usual sense, and almost none reached his advanced age of fifty.

He did refuse to accept them and he refused repeatedly. The three knelt before him regularly once a week, and once a week he passed on by with his eyes on the horizon. So, adding strategy to respect, they took to kneeling directly in his path. After the loss of much dignity picking his way among young backs, the Master Swordsman was forced to notice them in self-defense. His first words seemed to end the matter before it began: "Have your parents consented? When they do, I shall listen to your applications."

But boys of eleven, like girls of any age, are infinitely seductive. The tragic air of their complaints reminded the six parents that these were babies still, and that childhood imperatives are far briefer than childhood. They met in a Congress on

Boys and mulled the question: Why not end the clamor with a few bruises from the Master himself? A dozen adept whacks over the head would certainly end the dream more abruptly than increased work in the field. The six agreed, men in the front room, women in the kitchen, and all fell to talking about the Rout of the Minamoto over a sip of rice wine.

Yet the Old Swordsman, like many bachelors, knew more of the hearts of boys than their ever despairing parents who know only their young behinds. He knew this was neither a childhood fancy nor brief. He saw the solemnity in their eyes as they beheld his sword, their consummate respect of his own person, and he knew that when they were alone on the mountain that they repeated old tales of *Bushido* to one another in soft voices.

He watched their religiously male young lives, saw their tremendous beauty, ripe bodies and shocking energy. And his heart cried out that such explosive life can prove joyous indifference to death only by courting it. With a passion that would have astonished their parents, he wanted to ruthlessly blot out the boys' worship of cold steel, to see them disillusioned in him and their magnificent fire drowned in farming.

Toward this end and this end only, the Old Swordsman accepted them as students. There followed a four-cornered love affair that was all sadism, all masochism. He defeated them with a dainty flick of his wooden practice sword, method-

浪
人

ically bruised and bloodied them, scorned the least hint of skill, taunted their mistakes, spat on their respect of him, and told them countless stories of stupid heroes who slashed to shreds other stupid heroes, and in turn were themselves opened wide to soak the indifferent earth.

The boys listened with wide eyes, and each determined to become a much wiser stupid hero. Eleven became twelve. Twelve became thirteen.

The Old Swordsman stretched tight his endurance attempting to utterly weary and discourage these infinitely energetic young boys. He flung deadly sarcasm into their faces as each stood embarrassed before his fellows, and gave them tasks that could not be done except at the expense of all else. He gave over all waking thought to his plot for destruction, and, helpless, saw himself devoured by this silent fury. Yet none broke and ran. They rose, wiped off the mud and looked up at him with trusting eyes that asked, "And *now*?"

In despair, he ordered them out of his practice hall as hopeless. They had just become fourteen.

The three returned each day and sat on the Old Swordsman's porch waiting for him to relent. One morning, unaware that he was home, the least talkative said, "He loves us and our blundering can only show him that none of us would live past that first real duel with steel. And he very kindly thinks that that would be a waste—as if all this has been just preparation and not living life itself. Now, when he takes us back, we must cease our childish play and finally begin to study, listen, work. None of us has yet really tried. If we had, we'd wear top-knots now and not be sitting on his porch. I intend to make him proud of me one day—even if I have to run away and learn by testing my skill with strangers on the road!"

Dropouts have always horrified teachers who feel their own institutions the best available—adding with preposterous modesty "at this time." The Old Swordsman instantly fled to the mountain for nine days, and examined his own wisdom carefully. Finally deciding that he himself had been the youngest of the four, he returned with grim determination putting heel-thuds in every step. If he couldn't save these boy-men from glorious vivisection, he would at least postpone it by making them the most superbly adept fools in the dress of samurai. He would set to work in dead earnest to divide all he knew, the whole of his life and the sum of his expefience, into three.

Without expression, the boys knelt before him. There was no reason to be delighted at the sight of him; they'd known that he would return. They rose and began to study in young fury. Without superfluity in word or gesture, the Old Swordsman taught them in that same cold fury. They practiced unremittingly like the quietly insane, as insanely welcomed hardship, and rose before each dawn to sit in meditation. Loved by themselves and authority, they were kind, honest and truthful. And, though they seldom laughed aloud, there was an immense zest in all they did.

With grave joy, the three exchanged seed, resolutely keeping their samurai oath of female abstinence with the ease of the inexperienced. Their oneness reminded the Old Swordsman of the legendary harpist of great skill who cut the strings of his harp upon the death of that lover who was his most skillful listener.

He sat in the shadows and watched them rush through their lives to that destination which is the twin of birth. They had become fifteen.

Each hour gave the three greater skill. Their names came to be known throughout *The Place of the Forgotten Name.* Then word spread south to *The Ox of the Tenth Verse,* then more south to *Hachiman's Hunger.* And beyond. Yet, as is proper, it never reached the practice hall.

Word came suddenly. The Old Swordsman's last remaining brother had been murdered in a village to the south where his little temple stood. He seemed to have invited his fate, but the fact remained that some wandering ronin had cut him clean in two for no really satisfactory reason.

Before the Old Swordsman could realize that this was supposed to be a loss, his three young students vanished. They left a short, respectful note. The three swords missing from Sensei's collection were, of course, only borrowed. They would be returned in honor. They regretted leaving without permission but time would brook no delay. And other such youthful expressions.

As if cleaved from head to heart, the man opened his mouth and gave a great and silent cry. While the note was still settling to the floor, he swept up his sword from its stand and set out down the path. He left food in a pot over the fire and the door open. For the first time since his initial duel, he was afraid.

The honor of being chosen. . . .

The old monk's grave was easy to find in the cemetery near the crossroad. The marker was a square post of wood so new that it was white, the color of death. Having paid their most careful respects to a man they'd never seen, the three youths went on to the village.

They were met by a quiet little crowd, given rice and directions, and gravely embarrassed by the awe and gratitude of these faded peasants. The village, too, had that terrible melancholy of a thousand

浪
人
25

others, a new melancholy just eight days old. They left as soon as decorum permitted.

Erect and silent, the three traveled to the next village south. Again they were expected. There was much rice and bowing, both of which they returned. Now there were detailed descriptions of the man they were seeking. The dimensions of his body, strength and evil far exceeded the excellence of heroes. They continued to the next village south and then to the next, and suspense immobilized the province as ice stills the surface of a river.

Each of the three tried desperately to be ignorant of the myriad prayers that followed them. Nor did they look directly at the hundreds of boys and young men who studied them with reverence. Still boys themselves, they felt a deep sadness at this universal envy of a man willing to work very hard. And the envy of their beautiful and terrible mission. The air shimmered with silent whispering: *One day I shall be a kind, good warrior dedicated to righting wrongs! The first chance I get.* Even mothers murmured: *If he has to leave us, let him leave like this, a pure, strong man with a cause as sublimely righteous.*

They went southward to another village, and then one more. It was here that they found him.

The countryside was terrorized. Offended at some imagined slight, the Ronin had set fire to the biggest house in the village and stood with drawn sword to prevent any attempts to put it out. Then he discovered a young farm girl working in the millet field after the others had fled. She was the most beautiful virgin in the province and had great expectations. Being a man who lived in a state of acceleration, the Ronin combined his initial greeting and an invitation to the horizontal in the same sentence. Instead of salivating, she spat in his face.

Laughing as if he were amused, he took her to the inn and tied her to a rafter by her long jet hair. Just the tips of her toes touched the earthen floor. Her refusal to weep or beg took the enjoyment out of his morning saké. Familiar with peasant propriety, he stripped her naked. A tempest of outrage swept the village; both men and women came in droves to peek through the shutters and be horrified.

He announced his intentions to the unseen audience in a loud, clear voice. This rude girl who shamed the most hospitable empire on earth, would hang from that rafter until she begged him politely to relieve the natural tension of her maidenhead. Time, of course, meant absolutely nothing to him; he was quite willing to stay here just as long as she was. And should any fool be rash enough to attempt her rescue, that man would find himself hanging beside her by his balls. He'd learned how to do this from the pirates of the Three Han.

At the time of the arrival of the three youths, the maiden had hung there a day, a night and now half of a second day, without food, water, tears or begging. The peasants' tension had stretched to the point of general irritation that she was detaining him in the village so long with her pointless stubbornness.

It should not be assumed that the Ronin enjoyed the situation. His vanity was deeply wounded that the girl should prefer torture to his offer of the Ultimate Gallantry. He longed to bathe but that would look like a gesture of compromise; she must take him as he was. His departure must signify to everyone in the region that she was no longer a virgin and, further, that she had asked him to change her condition.

But as her inert body turned slowly on the rope, and her large toes traced two circles in the dust, his astonishment rose like a reluctant sun. He found himself in the very uncomfortable position of understanding her pointless pride. There were times that he wanted to embrace her gently and whisper, "Just *ask* and I swear I'll leave the village at a run. For I am burdened with this same pride."

The fact was that he didn't really need her body, and anyway maidenheads are always more or less annoying.

The three youths were hurried in the back door of the Temple with reverence reserved for princes. There the best calligrapher among them wrote a formal request to the Great Lord of the Castle for permission to carry out their vendetta within the village precincts. It was denied immediately and emphatically. The Great Lord's reply expatiated at great length on the evils of private revenge and expressed the hope that they would do nothing dishonorable during his absence. Away for an indefinite stay at the Capital, he would be completely powerless to prevent them from disturbing the peace, casting reflections on his honor and ridding the realm of a vile beast. The letter ended with the wholly extraneous information that he and his entire court were departing this same day.

For weeks retainers would be hurrying back to the Castle for necessaries they hadn't had time to pack.

The three sent a second note to the Ronin himself. It requested his presence at the *Bridge of the Gentle River's Passing* at the Hour of the Tiger on the following day. The purpose of the meeting was to straighten out certain matters pertaining to the abrupt decease of an elderly monk in the fifth village north. They signed with the new Zen names given them by their teacher.

The Ronin's brows rose. He'd never heard of any of them. This could mean that they were all master swordsmen traveling under assumed names or fine new talent that he'd missed hearing of in his travels. He seemed more interested than concerned. He breathed deeply and sifted the air with his nose. There was no danger.

On an impulse, he tucked the letter between the girl's buttocks. A corner stuck out like an impudent little rabbit's tail. For some reason, the sight amused him. He began laughing uncontrollably, ended red-

浪
人

faced and gasping. No danger, no danger. He left the inn detailing loudly what would happen if the girl were touched.

Long before the Hour of the Tiger, the three young swordsmen arrived at the bridge, undressed and waded into the cold water to bathe as a samurai must before each test of his skill. They had allowed plenty of time to scrub one another, dry well, to dress properly according to all the rules and even meditate briefly before the Ronin was due.

Then they were still. The three stood naked in the water looking up at the big man on the bank between them and their swords. He grunted: "But you're just children! And as scared as a kid about to have his first piece!" At this implication of fear, one walked out of the water and straight up the bank to the Ronin, leaving glistening footprints on the rocks. The boy said, "When we have finished bathing and have dressed properly, you may choose your opponent from among us."

The Ronin looked up and down the glistening boy and grunted again: "But didn't your *sensei* ever tell you that courage and skill are not enough? Did he leave you to learn cunning from somebody like me?" There was a moment of stillness, then, his arms becoming a blur, he sliced the boy precisely in two. The blade went between the eyes, through the navel and finally separated one testicle from the other.

As the body divided and fell, the other two

scrambled up the bank. The first to reach his sword stared in dismay as his hands vanished from his wrists. He sank into a sitting position and watched intensely as the third swept up his sword and fought in naked fury.

The Ronin was pleased at the boy's skill and almost impatient when the young feet slipped in the mud and his own blade entered the exposed throat. A great gush of blood arced many feet through the air.

The sitting boy wept without shame and asked to die with odd words: "Please cut the harp strings. There is no more music." The Ronin grimaced. The sword blurred. The head rolled yard after yard down the bank and into the water. Only after several moments did the eyelids cease quivering, and the mouth was still.

The big man walked back into the village very much annoyed. How could any swordsman be so bad a teacher as theirs! It degraded *Bushido* and it wasn't really fair to the boys. As his irritation grew, he decided to have the girl when he got back— whether she asked him or not.

Of course, some fool had counted on the three boys winning and had cut her down. He'd expected that, but it came as a real surprise to see the girl still there. She was crouched naked in a corner with her long black hair covering pale flesh. He roared 浪 laughter when he saw that the little rabbit tail was 人 still there.

It seemed he'd never known such joy as when he covered her on the earthen floor. His great body thudded down on hers through all the hours of the morning, and her nails dug into his arms and back.

In those hours he realized that he had infinite power in all things. He could do anything he wished and nothing could stop him. His would be an astonishing destiny.

The gifts of hate. . . .

The ghosts of the dead day came out of the evening earth as mist. Between a sigh and a smile, and with a dish of saké poised before his mouth, the Ronin suddenly remembered. He rose with a roar and ran out into the road and off toward the Bridge of the Gentle River's Passing. They heard him curse himself as he went for neglecting something so important. For the first time in all his many warrior years, he had somehow forgotten to loot the dead.

And even as he'd risen roaring, he remembered glimpsing a very fine sword lying across some clothing on the grass; the second boy had reached for it. Now the memory of the beautiful weapon blazed before his eyes as he ran hoping hopelessly that it wasn't too late. He wanted that sword with a grand ferocity and he'd have it if he had to ransack every farmhouse in the province.

As if colliding with an invisible wall, he stopped abruptly at the bridge. The bodies were gone and the entire scene washed clean and raked neatly as a garden. And, though the spot was infinitely empty, he heard the air rustling with the villagers' hate of him as a blind man hears the noises of the city. He looked around him sharply. His nostrils flickered. Not a soul.

He took a deep breath, relaxed an inch shorter and stood looking down the bank at the water. An almost fond smile curved his lips at the memory of the blank surprise on the faces of those three naked boys. The smile faded and he shook his head at the inexcusable waste to be blamed almost wholly on their teacher. No, ignorance can never excuse a man's viciousness.

The air crackled. He spun around. Momentary fear rippled through him. He froze at what he saw. An old man was sitting cross-legged in the center of the open space as if he'd been there meditating for days. He held a smooth stone lightly in his wrinkled hand and the second sword lay on the ground beside him.

The ripple returned as the Ronin looked into those old eyes. Never had he seen such impersonal

浪

人

33

hate. In them, he saw his own square post of new wood as casually raised as a man tosses away a piece of blade-cleaning paper. The ripple became a tide: *I have died and there is celebration.*

He licked his lips and said loudly, "And what do *you* want, old turd? Vengeance for these rare babies that didn't happen to die of starvation?" There was no answer. He tried to glare the old man down. It couldn't be done. Those eyes were stone. In a burst of panic, he swept out his blade and slashed down at the old head.

With a gesture that seemed languidly slow and immortally casual, the old man merely raised the stone between thumb and forefinger to a point above his brow. It met the sword's arc. There was a shimmering twang. The sword stopped. The hand and arm had absorbed the entire blow without seeming to move. Then something glittered in the twilight air. It was a perfect half-circle of shining steel from the foible of the blade.

The Ronin stood staring at his castrated weapon, at the unwavering stone and at the arm of steel. His sword lowered and touched earth for the first time. The world wavered as if he were looking through heat-waves.

There was worse to come. The old eyes ceased to be stone. They came to warm and loving life. As if caught in an impoliteness, the old man quickly came forward on his knees, touched his forehead to the ground and said, "Please forgive me for that which I came to do!"

The big man stepped back as from an abyss. Amazement left no room for thought. And the old man continued to murmur more horrors: "Having glimpsed your secret just now, allow me to make a small and humble reparation. Please honor me by accepting this sword. It is said to be priceless. Please accept this little bag of gold. It may ease some small part of your journey, for you have a long, long way to go. And, most valuable of all, please accept the fish in my forest pool. If you sit but a moment, I will give them to you."

The Ronin wanted to run. Sick with confusion, it was as if he'd suddenly found himself back in that bewitched village. The earth tilted. He was about to slide off.

He lowered his knees and sat on his heels and listened. The old man spoke quietly and his eyes glowed with a genuine love that terrified the Ronin. He must run. He must run *now*. There wasn't a moment to lose.

He sat and listened.

"In my forest there is a pool and in the pool there are three golden carp. One lists and swims in downward circles. Soon he lies weightless on the bottom sand, and he is relished by the water snails who also want to live as he did. On the surface and under an undulating lily pad, dart five golden

浪
人

babies protected by the mother carp and threatened by the hungry father carp. Two of these escape and grow to maturity and themselves make young. One of these lives to a grand old age because he has been clever in sneaking babies away from their mothers. 'But,' he tells himself, 'I have made the swift ones swifter.'

"Now each day for many years, a boy has lain here looking into the depths of the pool and watching the countless little golden generations. Knowing that none have left the pool, he stares into the water and asks a passionate question: *How many fish are in this pool!* He cries the question into the darkness of the night knowing that it is a foolish one yet he is caught by its terrible pertinence. Now I give his question to you as my most precious gift. And be assured, as a possession that none can steal, its richness will last far longer than either sword or gold."

After a moment, the Old Man bowed again, rose and walked off into the gathering darkness.

Once the figure was gone, the Ronin recovered quickly. The old man was out of his mind. That was the only possible explanation.

The simple diagnosis elated him He jumped up, jingled the gold and whirred the precious blade through the softness of the air. It must have a name! He looked around and found it at his feet. The prince of blades would be "Weed Killer," a good companion to his short sword that he'd named, with the same exuberance, "Pecker Two."

The feel of the hilt in his two hands sent a conviction of almost supernatural power up his arms. Of *course* he'd gotten what he came here for! That and a bag of gold to boot! It was silly of him to have run all the way from the village. Oh, he was the darling of all the great and little gods, and knew in his inmost guts that something outrageously fine was in store for him.

And *soon.*

浪
人

A small extravagance. . . .

In the great Eastern Capital, there lived a lord of
middle importance. He was the subject of much
behind-the-sleeve humor because he held the con-
tentment of his wife to be of prime concern. At
times, he carried this uxoriousness to surprising
extremes. Few forgot that he had once given one
of his palaces a quarter turn so as to improve the
view from his lady's apartments.

An excess of ridicule was precluded by the fact
that his wife was unquestionably lovely in manner,
face and form, and downright beautiful at those
times of serenity when she seemed to be a portrait
of herself. Her very presence was a pool of peace
reminding those about her that this moment at hand
outweighs all that is past and to come, and is, in
fact, all that we possess. None who looked upon her

at these times were ever luminous again behind their sleeves about their lord.

Now, while this serenity was a refuge to men of lofty minds like her husband, it was a torment to many others. The lady received ceaseless notes from impassioned and anonymous courtiers who described her own virtues to her and threatened a variety of things if she didn't become impassioned about theirs. Had any signed their letters, she would have still passed them on to her husband and remained aloof.

The fan mail reached its climax when one writer delivered his letter in person, having become so unhinged by her remoteness that he actually stepped behind her personal screen on the Moon Viewing Porch where she was avoiding the sun under a large hat and many veils. Without seeing her face but shattered by her presence, he touched his forehead to the hem of her robe and remained prone, murmuring extravagances. Her ladies in attendance could be heard all over the Capital.

The position of her admirer was too great a temptation to resist. The Lady drew her pocket poniard, the *kaiken* which all noblewomen wore, and drove it into the back of his neck up to the hilt. Perhaps sustained by the pride of having been personally stabbed by his Beloved, the rash man took three days to die. The Lady herself remained in an exquisite swoon throughout the Hour of the Cock, a rare feat during such busy and exciting early evening hours. The entire Court sent messages of sympathy and commendation, while thrilling with hope that the dead man had been a very much alive lover.

She neither denied it nor ever wore the little knife again.

The whole trifling incident distressed the Lord exceedingly. It revealed clearly the need for expert and faithful attendants. He must immediately procure at least two female *naginata* experts as constant armed companions for his Lady. He spent the following day auditioning the advanced students of the Imperial Ladies' Fencing School. His distress receded in copious tea and the special excitement of fighting females.

He stayed and stayed, discussing with the Master such proper irrelevancies as the unusually large flights of cranes this season. The cool little ladies were going through all of their forms a second time when he rose reluctantly, indicated two ravishing and cold-eyed honor students, and left, making Noh-like compliments on the tea.

His wife bowed low after the formal presentation of the embroidered bodyguard. Undone by his own generosity, he didn't notice that she looked at her new companions with the same cold eyes with which they looked at her. He hurried off to his apartments blinded by the lump in his throat. For giving makes us love both ourselves and the victims of our gifts.

It was from these two lovely bodyguards that the

Lord first heard of the Ronin. History forces the assumption that his Lady needed no protection that night, for these two related the Ronin's story in their Lord's private apartments over saké in the very latest hours.

His eyes went wide as he heard how this astonishing warrior had been ambushed by three master swordsmen from the north and had defeated all of them in less time than it takes to tell it. And this was only the most recent of a long line of noble adventures in his search for a worthy lord. They were certain that he must be of a noble line himself and forced to flee his patrimony because of some misunderstanding with a cruel elder brother over a beautiful concubine.

When one began describing details of the person of the Ronin, the Lord asked if she had personally seen his swordsmanship. Both swallowed and said *No* twice, then sat looking at him steadily with their cool eyes. At this, he swallowed and remarked that surely such a master would be too grand for so modest a palace as this. They both said *No* many times to this and, for some reason, began opening his robe and making most efficient love, each to an assigned area.

Coincidentally, the Ronin just happened to be pausing in the Capital City at that time and proved to be available when summoned for an exploratory interview.

Oddly enough, the Lady protested and asked that

浪
人

the audience be canceled. Would not all this military build-up suggest to the idle Court that she daily teetered on the brink of rape? Furthermore, a master swordsman of this caliber might be one of those little extravagances that rouse the suspicions of a much overthrown Throne. At best, the talk would be most unpleasant and the attention enough to force one to take long trips faraway from the Palace.

The Lord listened to her words gravely. He counted silently up to ten twice to give the impression that he was debating the matter, then finally sent a second message to the Ronin that the interview was no longer necessary. The Lady bowed low and murmured that she was overwhelmed by his consideration, and he hurried off to his apartments with another great lump in his throat.

It came as a surprise to the entire Palace when the Ronin appeared for the audience anyway.

There was a great deal of whispered consternation, then the Lord shrugged and decided to at least take a look at this paragon before sending him on his way. He could handle the man very well with a few coins and no emotionalism.

The sight of the huge man striding down the audience hall came as a shock. Clean and in borrowed clothes, the Ronin was massively male, darkly dour and utterly forbidding. When he knelt, his half-bow came as an additional shock. He looked calmly at the Lord, and the Lord suddenly found himself very interested in the design of his oldest fan.

Then, as if inspired, the Lord thought to clap his hands for saké. Now they sat in silence drinking by turns. He wondered desperately how to tell a man of this magnitude that it was all a great big misunderstanding. They sat and the interview took on the aspect of a dual meditation.

At last the big man growled, "You need a sword in the Palace?" and the Lord answered quickly, "Yes, when can you start?" The Ronin shrugged, "Now?" The Lord nodded his head many times as if it were the attainment of all his desires.

The Lady sat motionless behind her viewing screen at the end of the hall. Her ladies kept glancing at her. When the word "Now?" came echoing up to her, she rose suddenly and left in that angry flurry, not of dry leaves but the autumn wind.

Thus the whole relationship was wrong from the very beginning. The Lord had been intimidated into doing something he expressly wished to avoid. He would never forgive this. Again the Lady bowed low and murmured that she was overwhelmed by his consideration, through delicately gritted teeth. And the new retainer completely lost respect for his Lord before their first meeting was over. This accidental noble could be intimidated by something as simple as silence, as easy as ice. He had hired an unworthy employer.

From this point on there would be nothing but

浪
人

the growing tension of three wounded prides, and an endless whispering behind sleeves.

The inevitable flaw. . . .

As everyone knows, the word "ronin" means literally *"wave-man."* It implies that the unattached warrior was tossed helplessly upon the seas of a cruel destiny. Roughly, this is comparable to looking on a tiger as a victim of his environment.

However, the thorough delinquency of the average ronin could be easily brought to an abrupt end by the shock of respectability concomitant with steady employment and the white-collar title of samurai. Even the beast now entertaining our vicious curiosities was not insensitive to respectability. Or, conversely, when the unveiled eye looks on respectability as a very real vice, it becomes inevitable that this particular ronin should have been instantly attracted to it.

He took one tour of the Palace, heard himself addressed as *sir* for the first time, listened to the rustle of his new clothes and dozed outside a sumptuous meal—and immediately became a humble employee. A glorious amnesia wiped out the fact that only yesterday would he have been utterly disgusted at the sight of such an easily bought man, and furious at the suggestion that he, too, had a price upon his balls.

Today is always an exception.

Yet there is something both exciting and satisfying in the spectacle of a great, strong and handsome young male who is both obedient and respectful. When he's well-dressed, sheer vertigo ensues.

In this case, his superiors of all sexes were positively enchanted by the humility gilding his every word and act. Only the Lord himself preserved his own first impression of the man's talented arrogance. But he was too absorbed in his wife and shogun—in that order—to notice the new employee's change of character. Had he, the newly converted samurai would have been promptly returned to the status of ronin before you could say Miyamoto Musashi. No one is reassured at the sight of humility in his bodyguard.

All others were roused to paeans of praise and erotic reverie by this great big handsome young retainer. All others but one. This was no less a person than the Lady of the Palace who allowed herself a single glance from a great distance and immediately forbade him to enter or approach the vast quarters of the Palace under her dominion. She went so far as to alienate everyone by flatly categorizing him as a

浪
人

dangerous beast which should be slaughtered without a moment's delay or gelded and put out of the Palace.

It is understandable that the new samurai should be deeply hurt that anyone could be so utterly right about his character on so little evidence. It is only natural that murderers prefer to be hanged rather than lynched. Furthermore, he hadn't even gotten a glimpse of his accuser. He stood forever damned by a faint shadow on a distant screen.

His distress assumed impressive proportions when he rose each morning to don fine clothes, to eat fine food in a great palace where he was loved and respected, and where he realized that, now in his youthful prime, he had more than he'd ever dared want or imagine. It was *then* that this one, this single flaw in all his astonished heaven became especially poignant. It was very much like having a pubic hair caught under one's foreskin while being crowned Emperor.

Instead of savoring his good fortune, he fell into the habit of pique at the Lady's silly enmity. It came to the point where—when some new honor came to him—he wanted to blurt out foolishly, "Yes, but the Lady doesn't like me!"

And the Court consoled him, resented her and wished the Lord were man enough to discipline his wife.

Then—because physical power is comfortable to court and policemen have countless genuflecting friends—Okasan in the kitchen planned making his favorite *sushi* tomorrow and the two lance corporals plotted how to get into his kimono during the next picnic and the Lord wondered how he could show off his new samurai to the Court to best advantage and three boys of the Palace discussed asking him to teach them the Sword and the old gatekeeper went to sleep remembering his friendly greeting and at least one virgin ran her fingers down lightly between her legs imagining they were his and a dog lay pressed against his door alert to every sound within. . . .

While he lay in the dark staring at the ceiling and picturing how good it would be to sweep aside her viewing screen and bend over and take her little throat in his hands . . . and *squeeze*.

Patterns on the pond. . . .

Let us consider frenzy. It can be brought to flower in any man. All carry its seed in dark innocence and wait, unknowing, for that independence which will allow them to convert it from mere civilized irritation into the full blown rage of kings and presidents, man's most primitive offices.

Fortunately, the reverse is also true. The lessening of independence subdues frenzy and very soon we have one more normal man given largely to the habit of control, just as he was once given largely to the habit of frenzy.

Irrefutable proof of these profundities lies in the manner in which the new samurai around the Palace decided to vanquish the Lady who had destroyed his serenity with hers.

He approached the problem in two ways, both compatible with respectability. The first smacked of a certain rudimentary intelligence. He secured permission to take up the study of court manners, language and ceremony. This may have destroyed the myth that he was a fugitive prince, but it gave him a new reason to be adored: he was divinely *earnest*. Proving a ravenous student, he threatened to mince his instructors if they omitted or misrepresented a single detail, thus anticipating the zeal of Lord Asano by many generations.

His second strategem was more brilliant than intelligent. Using his newly acquired courtliness as a cloak of invisibility, he began a systematic seduction of everyone in the Lady's dominions who might be useful to his purpose. Using his indefatigable talent as currency, he manfully paid his way up the social scale from serving maids, assistant governesses and guards, through Ladies-in-Attendance, key courtiers and minor ministers, to the Inner Circle which included the two cold-eyed Ladies of the Sword with whom he had originally started out on the streets of the Capital.

The interest of these two had lapsed when they saw him shaven and in fine clothes, but now they found it fashionable to join the ladies of the Inner Circle in being amused and pleasantly shocked at such peasant potence under the fine *hakama* of a gentleman of charm. They wagered on the length of time that he could continue before physical collapse—and upon how long it would take him to finally lay a hand on the wrong rump.

Almost forgetting the reason for this vast offensive, he laughed at the ease with which he manipulated their weaknesses by giving a mere splatter of his ocean, and they laughed at receiving such an ocean in return for merely boosting him along the way to certain disappointment and death. All guessed where he was going.

Utterly bathed, groomed and scented with his very successful Bitter Lilac, he sat behind a screen, past a veil, within a shadow. Soon she would appear in the gentle early evening, speak of the wonders of the little day to her small son and watch him hurry off to bed. Waiting for this sight, the new samurai asked himself, "And then what?"

The question came as a jolt. It had taken such an effort getting to the screen itself that he hadn't really given any thought to what came next.

Certainly, he was repelled at the idea of throwing himself at her feet and begging for her kind regard. It wasn't like him, she wouldn't like it and it left the back of his neck unprotected. Then should he simply sit and reason with her? He somehow couldn't picture that. He could tell her she was in grave danger of a plot of some kind, or ask her to intercede with some unwilling virgin or, if everything else failed, simply burst into one of her favorite songs.

He shifted on his chair and it struck him that this whole damned thing was just a little silly.

There was a rustling far down the hall and the sound of a child's voice in the next chamber. Panic. Having been made fatally cautious by the good fortune of position, he fled before the Lady made her appearance.

For the moment, his flight served a good purpose. Today the Lady inexplicably defied custom by entering the room from the opposite direction and passed the screen from its open side. She took her usual place, listened gravely to the child and watched him go. Then she departed in a hush of silk.

Not until three days later did she remark mildly to her closest Lady-in-Attendance, "The screen hid nothing and the chair was empty, yet around them hung a most unusual scent. Would you please be so kind as to discover its name for me?" In terror, the attendant bowed low and remained so minute after minute. At last the Lady exclaimed mildly, gently, softly, "Ah, then it *was* Bitter Lilac!"

For a long while she watched the wind make patterns on the pond, then she murmured, "Please tell my Lord that I would like to speak to him? Very soon?"

The young woman took her terror immediately to the new samurai, gasped out that they had been discovered and said an exceedingly moist farewell. In white robes she retired to a secluded spot and was midway in the act of *seppuku* before realizing she'd forgotten to deliver the message to her Lord. She crawled bleeding down the main hall of his suite but never reached his door.

There was a terrible silence in that part of the Palace. No one dared go to help her until they were quite sure it was too late.

Only for a moment did the new samurai think of escaping. He dismissed the idea at once. It was not only beneath him but impossible. Even he couldn't fight off whole armies, for one erring samurai was far more dangerous than a hundred raging ronin, and must be exterminated.

Then he said a long soft *Ahhhhhhh,* for it was suddenly quite clear that the only refuge in the universe was obviously behind the screen, past the veil and within the shadow.

浪
人

Softly, do not wake the child. . . .

A thousand little bells seemed to shimmer in the air
as he saw the Lady tilt her beautiful head and, with
the face of ultimate tenderness, stroke the child's
cheek. The little boy's lids closed over a gaze of
utter security and he soared over the cliffs of sleep.
She watched the still little face for many moments,
at last took a deep breath and leaned forward to
rise. Midway, she stopped. After several dead
seconds she sat back down with the child in her lap.
She had smelled the scent of Bitter Lilac.

Without looking up from the *tatami,* she whispered softly, gently, mildly, "For this second intru-
sion, you shall be dead before dawn."

There was a rustle behind the screen as of someone leaning forward. The deep voice whispered,
"But you sent for me!" She looked at the speaking
screen: "Who told you such a thing!" and the deep
voice came to her as if out of Hell: "You did. For
a messenger to your Lord, you picked the one
woman in your Pepper Court that you were sure

would come to me first." Her reply was instant and less soft, less gentle, less mild: "Knew! I have never been more astonished at what she did!"

The voice from behind the screen was relentless: "You came in by another door and did not know? You waited three long days to speak and did not know? You told her that you knew and did not know! And even now you not only consent to speak to me but argue!"

The Lady's answer was a mistake but inevitable. It was the whisper of consummate scorn: *"Peasant scum!"* Few other words could have so effectively stripped the respectability from the man behind the screen. With them, she told him that even were he to live, his well-fed life at Court was at an end. In this, she forgot an ancient maxim of her people: *Always leave your enemy a little hope: it will be his undoing.*

With an immensity of motion that belied its silence, the big warrior set aside the screen, strode to where she sat and, standing over her, clutched the back of her neck in one hand and with the other flung open his robe below the *obi*. He rammed her delicate face into his musky, unclothed loins and held it there as she choked and gasped for air. Unflattered by the swelling tribute to her beauty, she fought the nausea gushing up from the wells of good taste and refinement located somewhere in the abdomen. Disgusted, he released her and stepped away.

浪
人

There was heavy-breathing silence as he arranged the extrusion of his robe and she her hair with one free hand. Then a great thudding of feet came down the corridor and the Lord swooped into the room like a distressed bantam. His first words were to the samurai: "I am grateful that you have anticipated my Lady's need for protection in this house of strange violence." Turning to her and the child, he spoke more gently: "I'm afraid your First Lady-in-Attendance is permanently indisposed. I suggest that you retire to more complete seclusion for the remainder of the night." She started to rise without looking up.

The samurai hastened to lift both her and the child as if they were no more than dreams of silk. The Lord added, "If there is anything whatever that you wish, this samurai will see that it is promptly yours. Not another of my retainers is so universally trusted in the Palace. I shall desire him to replace your ladies in the next apartment for the present until I have thoroughly investigated this confusion in the women's courts." He turned to the young man towering above him and ordered. "Do not leave her alone for an instant!"

There was a full round of bowing and the two parties went their confused, frantic and strangely self-satisfied ways.

The child slept on without interruption.

Naturally, the Lady woke in the night as her gown was flung apart, her nakedness presented to the upper dark and her legs wedged apart by a very business-like knee.

And naturally, she was indisposed the next day. Remaining in bed, she lay motionless with opened eyes. Yet when her Lord knelt by her with anguish on his face, the Lady could not bring herself to destroy so kind a man with the words of what had happened in the night. She therefore deprecated her condition as a foolish female reaction to yesterday's crisis. He was relieved, for there had been another plague that year.

Before going, he gave numerous instructions as to her care, returned at midday with spirit-rousing herbs and details of their recipe, and came a third time to sit with her through the long evening never guessing that his presence was the cause of all her pain.

Before going for the night, he gave the young samurai in the next apartment a superfluity of orders and finally went sighing down the great hall.

Unseen, she wept, not for last night's shame but for tonight's that would come as surely as moon-set. The Palace grew quiet gradually. She lay waiting in terror that almost knew relief when the panel slid open and the great shadow descended on her. It eclipsed the stars and pounded like surf, stopped her cries with its tongue and soaked her in its sweat. And the hours seemed to hover about the bed without passing.

Her ladies were too near and too dazzled to even

浪
人

whisper among themselves. Their many little juices simmered. True, the whole situation had all the appearances of violation but surely that was to add to the deliciousness. One word from the Lady and this gorgeously rough young warrior would die the slowest death that the Palace dungeon could devise. But there was no word, no cry nor even whimper from the Inner Chamber. And next day there was no look of accusation.

The nights became a week, the weeks became a month, and the rape became custom.

Now, at last, the new samurai looked into his steel mirror, laughed gleefully clear in his very soul and shouted soundlessly, *"Now, I have everything, everything, everything!"*

He even winked at his shadow.

Such shouts are inadvisable. Not only is *everything* relative, but its seeming possession should be taken as a warning. For the Turning had now come and the Lady would initiate it with a most peculiar vengeance.

And unwittingly, for she would loose the *Yomi* hags with no more than a delicious tilt of her head to the sound of a thousand little bells.

These splendid sins. . . .

Most beautiful women become platitudes when violation—rather than workaday copulation—is the motive of their seduction. After hardly fifty repetitions of his rape, the durable retainer's ferocity abated somewhat. Then it vanished completely. That was the night he felt her hand stroking his back.

The small gesture alarmed him, as it properly should. In the span of her next lunar lassitude, he took the opportunity to reduce his violations to a single nightly attack. And, as the monotony of it all struck him full force, he cut his assaults down to every other night. From then on it was easy to become virtually monk-like and indulge her only two or three times a week out of some vague sense of duty to the Lady of his Lord.

As most men do in such a situation, he found the idea of foregoing such a beautiful and highly placed woman particularly satisfying to his ego. This asceticism, made possible by nothing more sublime than fatigue, has ever misled the male into thinking that his Independence has been regained, and that his temporarily neglected but ever present Integrity has been revitalized in the cleansing fires of lust.

Abstinence, the other means to this end, takes so long.

Though largely without individuality at this time, the Samurai did differ from most men in one way. This was candor. He came to recognize that his powerful urge to "possess" a woman had always been twin to an equally powerful need to be rid of that urge. Indeed, he saw that a man's incomparable euphoria after having been properly "relieved" indicates indisputably that rut is not comfortable. The more virile, the more he'd rather be a hunter in the wilds and "his own man," a most revealing phrase.

Thus it was that this Ronin could never really become a samurai. In the middle of a banquet, he would unexpectedly remember the day on the road that he had only three sour berries to eat and oh how good they tasted! But he was patient with his good fortune and reached for more than he wanted as if he guessed that all this was only a phase.

Then it was with uncomfortable surprise that he woke in the night as his robe was flung open and his legs uncrossed by two very business-like hands. He had never felt more naked, a purely male condition, for no woman can ever be more than nude. After effect followed cause, he lifted up the self-spitted woman and almost roughly set her aside making some ungracious remark about having to get up early in the morning.

Now began a most amazing counter-pursuit in which he himself was constantly cornered and their relationship used as blackmail to prolong it. Wherever he turned, he was confronted by an avid woman of his own creation who, like an addict, could forego a smile, a friendly touch, the affection of a word, but not this drop of violent dew.

No matter where he fled to sleep secretly in the night, those who had conspired to get him behind her screen, re-conspired to get her behind his. Her quick, trembling hands ripped bare his body and wrenched loose floods of unwilling "satisfaction."

There was no rest. His perfect world took on the mildew of fatigue. Without zest, relish or interest in anything but uninterrupted sleep, he woke again and again in the black hours giving up yet another gush of weary seed lured from its hiding by an insatiate little woman *of my own creation, of my own creation, of my own creation.* . . .

But then it is quite possible that sex and pleasure are erroneously related.

And, all the while, the Palace was a huge fly, prismed with ten thousand eyes. It was a forest of pine hushed through with ten thousand whispers, and a vast battlefield crammed with watching warriors pressed around a mortal duel of children. The lovers' secret was known by all but one small man, and her gigantic need seemed at times to risk even his discovery.

Then the Court moved to the Spring Palace and the Lady was so occupied that her hunger appeared to wane. Hastening to end it completely, the weary young retainer did an incredibly foolish thing. On slight pretext, he slapped her. He was aghast to see her sink to the floor, embrace his legs and weep. Then he distinctly heard this Lady of Serenity whispering over and over, "I love you, I love you, I love you!"

Of course, being what he was, the young man had no way of guessing that she had never spoken these words before to any man. But rubbing his stinging hand, he sensed gloomily that the situation had entered into a new phase.

In the dead of night, he crept from the Spring Palace and rode far into the mountains to the Peephole of Hell, a quiet retreat built around steaming springs and attended by only two ancients. Peace was all-pervading. He slept superbly in the clean, cold air, woke joyously at dawn and, snatching up a sword and kimono, ran down to the misting baths.

Horror thundered through him as he stared through the steam and saw her smiling up at him.

It was the first time he had ever seen her smile. It chilled his being. His impulse to turn and go was thwarted by her wet hands sliding up his legs. Soon he faced her in the water, weary but compliant, the victim of that which he treasured beyond all things: the simple fact of his gender.

Her smile remained. He found it more irritating than significant—until too late. There was activity out on the road. It was the Cortege. His eyes went wide. He whispered: "Spies?" and she replied with deadly simplicity, "Oh, no, I left a message that I was coming here." His eyes searched her face for several precious moments, then he jumped out of the water, grabbed sword and kimono and ran toward the door.

It began to slide open. He swung to one side and stood back to the wall.

The Lord entered alone and went directly to the Lady. He knelt at the edge of the pool and said softly, "Oh, you smile. You're well. I was afraid the illness had returned." She looked up at him in a pleasant little awe: "Always kind, my Lord is always, always kind."

He laughed self-consciously: "But it is not kind to care for the one you love. Just selfish. They're right to laugh at me behind their sleeves."

Her face became still: "I have caused their laughter."

He smiled and shook his head: "You have excused their laughter." He shifted his position: "But I must go before they begin to laugh again."

Her question was thoughtful "Go?"

He laughed again as if his question were a joke: "Don't you want me to?"

She said, "No, never."

Pleased but embarrassed, he laughed a little loudly: "But, my dear, I must *some*time leave this room!"

She smiled a sad little smile and tilted her head: "No, not really."

"But why not!"

Her eyes were never lovelier as she answered: *"Because you are kind."*

The sword took off his head while there was still love in his eyes and a smile on his lips. The naked samurai did not move until it stopped rolling and was still. No longer courtier, samurai and lover, the Ronin held the blade in steam and wiped it on the body's robe. His face was still for the first time since he'd come to the Palace. Her eyes slid like hands down his big body and fastened hungrily on his angry groins.

Without a word, he flung on his robe and left by a side door. The Lady waited only moments then went out by the entrance that her Lord had used. She gave instructions that he did not wish to be disturbed.

Nevertheless, they were hardly gone an hour before the kindly murder was discovered and enraged pursuit began.

The white fist of fortune. . . .

The honeymooners reached the Palace shortly before midday and only minutes ahead of the dead Lord's guard on foaming horses. The shortening of the gap between the two parties could be ascribed to the Lady who had never ridden before. Every *ri* or so, she decided that death at the hands of their pursuers would be preferable to what her horse had in mind. So she would periodically stop and submit herself to Fate, continuing only when her enraged companion rode on without her.

He didn't like horses either, having had only recent experience with them. Furthermore, the anatomy of his gender had far more to fear than that of the Lady whose very sex connoted the equestrian arts. Yet he preferred the risk of being gelded by a gelding to the Lady's company in pitched battle. He knew quite well that once they were encircled, she would weep, cling to his busy arms and fall down frequently as all the high-born heroines did in the love-tales of that day. And he

浪
人

knew exactly how radically he'd differ from the average hero when she did.

It was also the Lady's idea to drop in at the Spring Palace for more comfortable traveling clothes and ample traveling expenses. She'd heard those tales herself, and remembered clearly that fleeing lovers without collateral never seemed to get very far from the fiefs in which they were registered. When the Guard was sighted down the road, she was far more distressed at having no opportunity to change her clothes than failing to find a bag or two of *ryo* around. In great pique, she swept up a suede scrotum of rubies and fled with her seducer out the rear entrance just as their nemeses thundered in the main gate and awakened the Palace to horror.

The Great Female Sun slipped from the modesty of clouds and blazed nakedly upon a scene of gratifying confusion, for as long as men are stupid they will need stupid gods. The angry panic within the gates contrasted with the dark pair picking their way down the dainty and intricate paths to the river. The Lady seemed to jog and stumble as well on foot as on horseback; she had never walked much before either. So it was her gait as much as her gown that drew attention from the Palace walls. There was a cry within, a pointing finger and a flinging wide of the several river doors. An avalanche of avengers swept down the slope toward them as they reached the Landing.

There were several frail boats tied along the pier.

On his order, the Lady went ahead with adorably slow and mincing steps, and attempted untying this rope and that with noble ineptitude. The Samurai stood at the head of the pier facing their pursuers. As if he'd almost forgotten, he began pulling up his sleeves. The avalanche slowed and stopped. He deliberately looped the shoulder strings around the big sleeves and even arranged a few folds. There was no movement on slope or shore, nothing to be heard but the ignorant river-birds and the fragile little grunts of the tugging Lady.

Both sleeves out of the way, the Samurai wiped his hands on his thighs and held them up with fingers spread wide as if to see how steady they were. All eyes went to them. They were like rock. Their startling steadiness was one of the things that most of the survivors remembered.

They also remembered how he drew and slashed with a single movement. The arm of a man before him dropped out of its sleeve. The man looked down at it in surprise, then he frowned and began to moan softly. When he finally screamed, a hellish scene exploded upon the slopes of the Great River.

The unthinking mob surged forward from behind shouting slogan-like sentiments about their late Lord's apparently untimely death. This forced their unwilling leaders directly into the mill of the Sword at the head of the pier. Without moving his feet, the Samurai made figures in the air with his shining blade which each felled two and sometimes

浪
人

three of the closest observers. None were adversaries; none had a chance to fight. This was no contest, for it is wiser than brave to be one against one hundred.

The tiny grunts behind him indicated that the Lady was more interested in confirming her background than her future. He backed out onto the pier and somehow ordered her into a small covered boat without raising his voice. She crawled into it awkwardly and huddled trembling under the little roof.

The swordsman stood with legs spread, knees slightly bent and sword pointed straight ahead. His eyes began to widen and glare like Bodhidharma on a scroll. Three moments after the pause had become intolerable, he uttered a terrifying *kiai* with wide open mouth and bared white teeth, and charged.

A retreat took place.

His sword touched no one in the ebb of that vast human tide, but there were broken bones, cracked ribs and many concussions. Having destroyed them with themselves, he walked back down the pier, got into the boat, untied the rope and stood in the bow wiping his blade clean as they drifted slowly out into the river. There was a long pole. He dug it into the muddy bottom and the boat surged forward into the swifter current in the middle of the river.

Pursuit hesitated. It was pointless wasting arrows at that distance, and running along the shore would look a little foolish. Naturally they must send a rider on to the next landing. The arrows there might have more effect, for the river would have narrowed. And naturally that would suggest to the flying pair that they look for landings on the other side of the river. Perhaps this terrible pair would be lulled if a rider were not sent and nothing happened at the next landing. Then they might be lured into the sudden rapids immediately beyond.

A general *Ahhhhhhh* arose. No one had ever ridden those rapids and survived. And, if by some miracle they should, the next daimyo had a heavy net going from shore to shore for boatmen trying to elude his river highway toll.

There was a thoughtful silence among the avengers. Apparently the gods were taking the whole matter out of their hands. They'd tried their best and, though they'd failed their dead Lord, Vengeance would be done nonetheless. Everyone went slowly home feeling rather good about the whole affair. In deep mourning, of course, but feeling rather good.

The river narrowed, grew swift and the next landing was going by before they noticed it. The little boat leaped forward in an almost gleefully vicious rush. Soon it seemed to be falling through space. They careened insanely. The universe was nothing but a terrible noise.

The madness of those about to die undoubtedly means nothing. The young warrior simply grasped

浪
人
67

either side of the boat and stared ahead. The Lady, on the contrary, crouched on the bottom and screamed frightful obscenities at him. He gave no indication of hearing.

Finally, as if struck by a great white fist, the boat shattered against a rock.

In the white chaos, he seemed to hear his own voice shouting up from the bottom of a milky well, *"Ronin, ronin again!"* It seemed pleased. There was another voice, too. Within the crashing and the thunder, some fool murmured across a vast distance, *"How many fish are in the forest pool?"* It seemed friendly.

After gigantic noise, awful peace. He lay on sand. No bed had ever felt better. He opened his eyes and looked at the still and solid world. It was good. He sat up slowly and saw her sitting on a rock some distance away. She looked up and said without an excess of interest, "Oh, I thought you were dead."

Inventory revealed that neither was hurt, that Weed Killer lay unharmed in the shallows and that the little bag of rubies was still safe inside her belt. They'd lost nothing but their shoes and Pecker Two. He laughed. The great luck was still with him. She looked at him with disgust and grunted in a way that ladies never grunt. He insisted that they were the darlings of the gods, having escaped without loss or injury, and those rubies were wealth enough to keep them well fed for generations.

She looked at him with disgust again then out

over the river and said, "Have you ever tried to pay for a bowl of rice with a ruby?"

A delicious tilt of her head. . . .

They found the Highway and followed it on bare and tender feet. When the sun was directly overhead, they came to a certain small village. It was so utterly dilapidated that both refugees knew instantly how preposterous it would be to give the smallest of their rubies for the entire village and its inhabitants, much less a meal or a hundred thousand meals. So, wealthy beyond measure, they found themselves bowing humbly and begging for food in the peculiarly pained humility of a millionaire who has only a hundred dollar bill to pay the cab fare.

In love tales, the wise peasants always see through the rags of disguised nobility at once. Legend tells us that they are always much taken with the Fleeing Princess and her Handsome, Distressed Lover whom 浪 they care for tenderly at the risk of their lives as if 人 aware that this is only the penultimate chapter and the glorious showdown is yet to come. In actual practice, they are likely to act somewhat differently. In this case, they snorted at the woman who was obviously a madam and at her great, hulking pimp who wore a sword illegally as if he were a real samurai. She might think she was bowing but the movement gave the impression that she had a stiff neck which allowed her to unbend only a quarter of an inch to peasants and hardly twice that to the chief men of the village. They unanimously refused to sustain the woman's affected airs with a single grain of rice. Let her eat millet—preferably somewhere else.

The whole experience shattered the Lady. To be refused the most basic of necessities by the very serfs that Heaven had put here on the Eight Islands to serve her, was profoundly shocking—and so coldly infuriating that everyone in the province would have left for Hokkaido in panic had they guessed only a few of the vengeances that passed her mind.

However, she was essentially a practical woman. Examining their appearances and behavior with admirable objectivity, she decided that the whole trouble lay in her escort's sword. At her insistence and contrary to all he held wise and holy, he left his steel soul hidden in brush at the outskirts of the next village. Now, he would not be tempted to use it to extort food as he had been in that last place. Not only she but the peasants had seen his black anger and his hand masturbating the handle of his sword. No more of that. She was satiate with violence and certainly had no intention of stealing food however hungry they might get. This time they would give the peasants' better natures full opportunity to well up and shower them with comforts, as they must when they detected her nobility.

They didn't eat in this second village either.

After the first dozen indecent proposals, she raised her head proudly and led the way out of town. Waiting outside the last little house, she primped pathetically while the Samurai ran back for his sword. In this house lived a small and willowy bachelor. Helplessly dazzled by the huge warrior, he shared his scant store of food with them. It was supposed to have lasted for the week, but the minutes of its going were merry ones. Silly as he knew it was, he pretended to himself that she was a Princess fleeing with her Lover, and he served her tenderly like a wise and loving peasant. When his pretty guests had gone, he found that his tiny hoard of pennies had gone with them. Alone in his little house, he wept a while, sighed a few times and went back to work.

Traveling from village to village, they found no one to buy the least of their rubies. They sought out that lowest of all classes, the merchants, who ranked just slightly above the Eta who weren't really people at all. But merchants are few in the country and those they did meet were suspicious of both the

浪
人

stones and the means by which they'd been obtained. Quotations ran satirically low. The Lady strode away in regal anger refusing to part with a single jewel for less than its full value, whatever that might be.

Around this time, she began to complain. She had numerous aches and there was horrid sunburn, filth, flies and fleas, and she never got a good night's rest on a bed of straw. Her whimper followed them like a dog. Yet it was she who kept them together with her granite conviction that they would eventually find a place of respect for herself, her jewels and her samurai. She constantly reminded him that he was indeed still her retainer and could expect most satisfactory rewards for his fidelity.

For some reason that was yet to bubble to the surface, he stayed and protected her on the journey as if in some thrall. Without surprise, he watched them become, in time, beggars by profession, schemers by necessity and prostitutes by indolence. Galled by her refusal to let him win their way with his sword, he still stayed on and tried to cope with this slowly growing nebula of nausea in his middle as he bowed in begging, stooped to pick up coins after a show of sword tricks for the rustics, or lay with his robe raised and parted with morsels of marrow for the sad little cashes of matron and maid, merchant and monk.

He wondered at the way she seemed so aloof of those who bounced upon her middle; at first silent, she came to discuss her customers as poor fools and the damned, never once applying the description to herself. Just a little time ago the Lady of a Palace, she seemed a little amused that all these silly men would pay for something that it cost her nothing to give.

Though she took a certain efficient pride in their mutual whoredom, she was capable of great anger when catching him at theft. It was not only Wrong but Risky, and she would not have it. He snarled and took a deep breath, for he knew what was coming yet again. Once more he'd tell her he had no intention of begging all his life and why the hell didn't they go to a good-sized town for once, sell a stone for whatever they could get and have a good meal, a hot bath and put on some clean clothes! At these times, she screamed. Those wretched little red stones were all she had left of Lord and Palace, Child, Position and Name, and she would not risk a single one of them! They were *her* rubies and *she* would decide their disposition without suggestions from the very lackey who had brought her to this degraded state.

She kept touching the place where the little bag was bound underneath her belt. The gesture had become an established habit with the unconsciousness of a tic and the pathos of an unwittingly revealed anxiety. He remembered her serenity the day he'd watched from behind the screen. She'd tilted her head and so gently stroked the baby's cheek.

Never had there been such beauty. Now he watched her methodically destroy every trace of it.

One night he got them a little room and some saké, and made love to her for the first time since their flight. She looked at him sideways and said many times. "Stop it, you're being tiresome!" but kept touching her hair. And she kept saying, "You know very well I detest getting drunk!" but let him fill her flat little bowl and ran each sip around in her mouth before she swallowed it. He began to act very foolishly so she wouldn't think that she was getting drunk alone. He imitated customers, and said vulgar things that she usually forbade but now laughed at. They sang and remembered funny little things about the Palace, absurdities and the unpleasant, but nothing grand that would betray their profound regret at having undertaken this dark adventure. At last they lay together in numb and sexless sleep.

He woke and lay still long minutes to be sure that she still slept. Her breathing was regular, slightly whimpering and just the smallest bit vulgar. He slid his hand under her belt and slowly, slowly drew out the little suede bag. He reached into it with only finger and thumb for he intended taking just one or two. He squinted at the stones and went over to the wick burning sadly in the bowl of oil. He stared and poured all of the stones into his palm. They were milkwhite pebbles.

He looked at her still form. Which of all of her

wretchedly self-effacing customers had offered saké, too? Which had been so generous that she took heart and did not hate her life and let him pour yet another dish of wine? Months ago, he remembered her laughing with someone behind closed doors in some dismal inn. Months ago and she hadn't looked into the bag since but had only felt it and gone on worrying night and day about a treasure she no longer possessed.

He must go. The discovery would be a catastrophe that would bind them together forever. Nor could he bear the thought of seeing her face after she knew.

He must go, yet not tonight. She'd think he'd gotten her drunk and had stolen them himself. Tomorrow.

The next day she smiled at him and scolded quietly; their little party had been an extravagance but she felt much better. She laughed at the memory of him making such a fool of himself: "If you only knew the silly things you did last night!" He shrugged and couldn't look at her. He'd wait a few days.

They passed and with them weeks and months, and each morning he rose knowing that today she might decide to open the little bag and pour out the little white seeds of death into her palm. Hope would die and he'd never be able to go again.

Then it happened.

A thousand little bells seemed to shimmer in the

浪
人

air as he watched her tilt her head deliciously and reach for the peasant child with a wonder of tenderness. And, even as his heart leaped with silver echoes, she dug her fingers into the little arms and hissed, *"Who cares if you're hungry! If I ever catch you around our food again, I'll scratch your shitty little eyes out!"*

Something came to the surface and burst in uncertain thunder. He stood suddenly and knew that all of this was over. He began walking but unaware of direction, for his whole being was caught up in great battle.

He walked and walked, trying desperately to push Something away. It was a power as great as the sky. Then, as he fought, it began to make itself clear and panic took him. This time he would not survive the Great White Fist. The shape resolved itself into sound, and he knew that he was fighting passionately not to hear three terrible words. They must not be uttered! His role as Darling of the Gods, his strength and manhood, his name and very place in the Universe depended upon not hearing those three ghastly words.

Then the stars went out and it was over. Far out in a black field, he stopped without knowing he stopped and gave up all he held dear, all that was to come, his hope and his very name in an agony of midnight joy.

As he plunged into Hell, the Ronin screamed those three eternally damning words, "I DID IT!"

The wave-tossed man. . . .

He ran, stumbled, fell and rose and ran. In a world with only two directions, he simply ran *Away*. In a universe against which there was no defense, he ran without his sword. Unaware that he had flung it away, flung away his sharp and shining soul of steel. All he knew was that he was free of some encumbrance and that he must hurry.

His lungs screamed for rest but he ran without pause. Cut and bleeding, he ran through the sharp-forest, into the leech-filled, addered marshes, deeper and deeper into the despairing wasteland that has no farther side.

He was lying full-length, his great weight crushing itself upon nettles and his flesh feeling nothing but a black appropriateness. He lay knowing only the vast surprise of those three words, their deadly discovery and their finality. He wept with weariness but could not sleep. His throat was molten and there was the sound of near water, but he had no will to move nor to stop his lips that moved endlessly in forming the Words, *"I did it!"*

浪
人

Not sleep but a dream, and his burning eyes were seared with sights he'd once beheld but had never seen.

The little old monk lay in halves in the lazy dust and chuckled to himself as he tried to scoop up his own blood with old, cupped hands.

Three naked boys, all trace of maleness hacked away, stood knee-deep in a river of their own blood and stared up the bank at him with eyes of white stone.

The virgin hung by her hair and winked at him lasciviously as she fingered herself.

The Lord's head laughed tremendously as it rolled swiftly toward him through steam, and the Lady, plucked out the child's eyes with exquisite tenderness, and put them in a little leather bag.

None made a sound, yet there would never again be Silence because there were words forever graven on the air: *I've been told that the samurai who has never died is apt to run and hide in decisive moments* and that small, old voice saying, *You are still under arrest* and the most outrageous of all *How many fish are in the forest pool?*

He ended this Congress of Hell with a great cry, stumbled to his feet and ran on through the gray dew of dawn. But no longer *Away*. Now he clutched at a terrible need that he had fashioned to die by: "I must get there before the bell sounds! The year is up and now it is almost the Hour of the Ram!"

The word "urgent" exploded before him like lightning and the crumpled letter cleaved to his throat like a throttling hand.

He ran up the North Highway and back through time with staring eyes and opened lips. The peasants paused in their work to watch him fly past the landmarks of all his crimes and hasten to the spot of lazy dust. Never stopping day or night until he fell and could move no more, he waited out the revival of his body in a circle of his own personal ghouls that rustled to him through dry grasses and stood watching his helplessness with crashing silence in their eyes.

He ate leaves, he ate roots, he ate weeds and his dead tongue tasted nothing. He drank any water that called his eyes with glitter and hurried on his dark way talking, mumbling, urging himself like a horse through villages where he had once strode in proud violence.

Little faces stared startled at the frightful spectacle of a man caught in a damnation that he had made and that they had prayed for.

Once a child's voice pierced his haunted race: "Father, why is the samurai crying?" As if discovering something unclean about himself, he felt his head, ran into the nearest house for a knife, and slashed off his top-knot and flung it into the fire. It sizzled and made a pungent little stink. They stared from corners, petrified at this most incredible of all acts, and went on staring into the fire long after the

浪
人

madman had loped out of sight upon the North Highway.

On and on, slower and slower in the dream-despair of a man running underwater. He wavered from one side of the road to the other, slid down the banks and clambered back up as if the Highway were a moving thing that would take him to the needed place.

Slower and slower. His battle with space became a barter for inches.

Then parts of an inch.

At last he stopped and merely stood. There was nothing left, not even the energy to fall.

And, as he stood on the vast plain, the silent ax descended. He crumpled like cloth into the dry grass and lay motionless in a death of sleep. The day, the night and another day passed over him, and he made no sign of living. Night rolled over him and, in the darkness, the fingers of one hand stirred.

When he woke, it was indeed the Hour of the Ram and the year was up, and he lay at the crossroad outside the bewitched village.

And the writer of the letter was bending over him with a cup of steaming tea.

Instructions to a dead samurai. . . .

He sat up painfully and knew, without caring,
that he was no longer young. He looked at the life-
giving steam with dull eyes. When the cup came
closer, he did not move to take it. His gaze traveled
listlessly to the little fire and the iron pot over it. His
voice was not so deep, nor yet a growl as he asked
the little flames, "How can I be forgiven?" The cup
moved closer. Ignoring it, he looked up and repeated the question earnestly like a young boy. No
longer young nor enchanted with his own crotch-
prime, the youthfulness became him.

The reply flicked him as a giddy riddle: "This
cup brims with the answer." He grunted with weak
disgust at the playful obscurity. Then a wisp of the
steam insinuated itself upon an inhalation and
whispered to his body to rise against him. He took
the cup as out of duty. His shaking hand made
inward rushing circles on the surface of the answer. 浪
His nostrils flickered and his eyes widened in the 人
terror that all dead men feel who are about to drink *81*

the poison that will bring them back to life again.

He was startled to feel the hot, stinging amber rush into every part of his dormant body. He sat and there was a quiet singing. For the first time, he was not deceived by this melody. He took a second sip and knew that the answer had been neither giddy nor a riddle—nor pleasant. *The first step to forgiveness is living.*

As if the words had been spoken, he looked up at the peaceful eyes and demanded with the strong voice of the tea: "I'm not interested in living! I want only to be forgiven!"

The voice was matter-of-fact: "To forgive is to condone. Could you worship any god or gods who would condone what you have done?"

His answer came instantly with the remembered ferocity of a ronin: "*Never!*" Then he seemed to crumple: "Yes, yes, I knew there would be no forgiveness."

"But of course there is!"

His eyes glittered angrily as if he were being played with: "Where?"

"If I weren't here, you'd answer that yourself! You can be forgiven only by the ghost of each living thing that you have killed."

"Ghost! *You* believe in ghosts?"

"After listening to your cries as you slept, I *have* to believe in ghosts!"

The man on the ground became as earnest as a boy again: "But—but how can I go to them except by dying? Are you saying that I must kill myself? I will if you tell me to."

"Drink your tea."

He sipped noisily then looked up and asked, "Should I go to witches?"

"Oh, Fool, Fool, let the dead come to you! Haven't they always? Why should they stop now!"

He was bemused: "Yes, let them come forever."

"I'm sorry but that's not possible at this time. Ghosts aren't allowed to haunt other ghosts. Just living people. And, in the meantime, I suggest you get to your fish."

He looked away in irritation: "Oh those goddam fish. They follow me worse than the ghosts. A silly damned riddle in the middle of a time of tears, and I can't get it out of my mind!"

"Oh, you are so fortunate to be haunted by all these beautiful ghosts. Without them you'd never, never attain Damnation!"

The man on the ground said, "It's fun to you! A man crawls to your feet in agony and you make precious little jokes. *I need help!* Where is this goddamn forest with the old man's pool? Do you know?"

"No, but you do. If you'd only listen to what you say instead of talking so much! You know very well the only way to get there is to follow a blind man with no legs."

The big warrior covered his face with grimy hands, rocked back and forth and moaned: "I beg for help as I've never begged before and you smile and give me shit! I'd do better to sit in front of a blank wall and stare!"

The other laughed aloud: "Excellent, excellent! That's precisely what you must do! I knew you knew! What am I doing here but serving tea! Have another cup! The second is never, never like the first."

There was a patch of quiet. The man on the ground sipped without tasting, looked out over the plain and asked, "Sensei, will I ever sleep again?"

"No, not right away. Perhaps in years to come. You've been asleep so long that now you're awake you won't want to miss a moment. The awful pleasure will make you thin, but in time you'll earn little snatches of oblivion. Yet your search for them will be that of a man clawing his way through a mountain of rock with no tool but his bloody hands."

He whispered: "Then what's the purpose?"

"*To get to the other side!* Even a child knows that a man with only bloody hands and a few tears has more purpose than any mountain of rock! I must go. I'm a thousand words too late already. Wisdom is never transmitted through the mouth."

He began putting out the fire. The man on the ground struggled about in the lazy dust to face him. There was desperation on his dirty, tear-stained face.

He said, "No, Sensei, no, no!" and his voice was

light and rapid as a boy's. "There are so many things that you must tell me! My life's been shattered by a rosary of riddles that you must solve! The village was bewitched; how could this be? Why did the Old Monk make me kill him and how could you write that letter unless you knew that I might come? What was it that surprised the Old Swordsman when he looked at me? More than any man I've ever faced, he wanted to kill me. Then he looked in my eyes and was amazed and gave me everything he owned. And all of it, the Gifts of Hate, like when you give a vat of wine to a man you know will drink himself to death. The bastard pitied me! How could he know I'd be crawling here in dust today! Yes, and the other at the Inn: he said, We thought you might be different—*our scout was sure you were.* How so different a dozen *ri* away? How marked? And what is there that I'm supposed to do? A strange election's taken place and I've been chosen to act out some Mystery without a single When or Where or Why!"

He stopped for breath and added, "I know a riddle that has an answer is no riddle, and a life with no questions is no life, but these pound each of my seconds into dust and with them that squirming little core I call Myself."

He swallowed and sifted dust through unfeeling fingers and, having cried out the heart of the matter, tapered off with trivia. For a man does not stop his words abruptly. "And will I always feel this dry,

浪
人

this dead, this cut off from the whole of Man? Like the Old Monk said, I'm still, still under arrest and my sword's been whisked away. I was all hunger just a little while ago, any hunger you can name. Now not a one." He abruptly lifted his head to the sky and whispered: *"How did she know she mustn't look into the little leather bag?"*

Then back with a light voice and infinite apathy: "Now not a one, not a single one! And I don't trust a sudden thing. I learned the Sword in slow pain like a baby's born. The labor lasted years and today I bore a bubble." The tones sank to a sigh: "And if I'm good and never do another evil thing, I'll still go to hell, won't I, Sensei? I mean, you can't be only partly damned, can you? And there *is* a Hell, Sensei, there *is?"*

"You live the answer and yet you ask. Talk on, talk on, and you'll answer all you want to know."

"There is. Then, whatever Death may be, it must be good."

Hot tea splashed in his face. He groaned and fell backward, and the voice said, "Idiot, *death is none of your affair!* Now, stop all these masturbating questions and get to work!"

He wiped the burning wetness from his face: "Work? What work, Sensei?" In the silence he saw *kanji* written in the dust with a little twig; they said, with the seeming irrelevancy of the really apt, *The Grand Capacity to Do and Suffer.* And a voice whispered on the cool breeze against his face, "When life is more terrible than death, then it is the truest valor to dare to live."

He held still while the words seeped into him, then he woke with a jerk and looked about him. The Teacher was already far off down the road carrying the iron pot carefully so as not to spill the remaining tea.

Sitting in the dust, he cried out, "What shall I *do*, Sensei?" and the voice came back to him as down a long tunnel through a great mountain:

"Become a *real* ronin!"

The Sun rose, and the world was filled with sight enough and sound to deceive all but the deaf and blind and wise.

浪
人

87

Rage and adoration. .

The boy watched the historic Fight on the Landing
in terror, of course, because on this day both parents
were vanishing from his life. But he also watched in
a certain amazement, the ferocity of the lone man
holding off the arms of the entire Palace with only
Weed Killer. He didn't so much as touch Pecker
Two. The boy had reverently handled both.

So, in spite of the fact that his father lay beheaded
at the Peephole of Hell and his mother was being
ruthlessly abducted upon the wide river, the scene
that remained seared into his mind was that of a
single figure with bared teeth, eyes wildly intent and
movements as precise as they were economical.

The long blade was not mere opposition to all the
Guard. It was Punishment and, as such, gave majesty
to the Criminal.

The boy's hating wonder gave birth to a wish.

The wish bore a resolution and that became a Vow. In an agony of contradiction, he knew that one day he must kill this hideous man with the same courage, skill and grandeur that he now beheld upon the Landing. The Vow was a permanent part of him before the little covered boat was out of sight around the bend of the great river taking with it all he held to be Good and Evil.

As well as his Mother.

The Palace dissolved. With neither Lord nor Lady nor a regent for the young Daimyo acceptable to all, both relations and retainers went their ways to survive and thrive and die elsewhere. The Palace, once forbidden to all but the Select, became the home of wind and web, and bird and bee.

The boy himself was swept up by a paternal uncle, the daimyo of a province to the north. With grave delight at this gift of a precious little manchild, the humiliated father of nine daughters immediately adopted him as son and heir. And at the earliest opportunity stripped him bare and paid delighted reverence to the little pod with two peas in which hung the future of his realm.

In addition to the doting, the Uncle made a second mistake right at the beginning, that time of greatest danger. He solemnly revealed to the child that his Father had flagrantly invited death and that his Mother had herself done the abducting.

Because the truth is seldom self-apparent, the effect of this information upon the child was instant

浪
人

detestation of a lying benefactor. He knew very well that both of his parents were unquestionably Perfect as well as Beautiful.

After two years of excessive pampering, the seven-year-old prince announced that he was going to become a great swordsman as of Monday. There was unanimous approbation, from the Daimyo himself down to the assistant wood-gatherers. A full day before Monday, an expert teacher came to live at the Palace and to give the child daily lessons in the rudiments of *kendo*. There was much attention paid to costume and the appurtenances. Everyone admired the child and he became one degree more insufferable.

However, the teacher treated this seven year old as a child, of all things, and conducted his lessons in utter dread of so much as scratching the great Daimyo's new and desperately beloved son. The child, incapable of communicating nuance, declared that this good friend of his welfare was an enemy of his future—which seemed at the time to be just around the corner. Summing up the delicacy of the entire situation he used the words, "I hate him!" and the puzzled teacher was packed off with a great deal of coolness.

The replacement naturally fell into the same error. In fact, warned by his predecessor, he treated the young warrior even more like a child and took even greater care against accidents. His was a travesty of respect and the meticulous, in spite of the child's obvious hunger to learn and his indifference to being hurt in the process. He went quickly, unaware that the child had taught him that the most valuable lessons come only once.

Two years passed and with them eleven teachers. All came in eagerness and left in nonplus. The Uncle nodded in amazed pleasure: "Only a baby and already a warrior!"

He was a little less pleased, though still amazed, when the child heard of a master swordsman who had retired far into the mountains, and decided to retire with him. The boy ordered a box of *kashi* and *sushi* to be packed, stuck his wooden practice sword in his belt and left the Palace as if he loved no one, so complete was his omission of goodbyes.

Of course, his journey took no one by surprise. The lone boy strode up the mountain invisibly attended by a full guard, whole banquets of food, wardrobes of clothes and a selection of his favorite toys.

Unaware of all this, he finished the last of his *sushi*, walked into a monastery, demanded the special of the day which happened to be thin rice soup, drank it in silence and departed without the faintest expression of gratitude. When the Directors of the Stealthy Retinue attempted to thank the head monk more concretely, they were met with a most abrupt rebuff: "Since when must we thank someone for feeding us when we are hungry? Send our thanks to the Child."

浪
人

Although this sort of thing is expected of religious people, it became cherished legend and the monastery—after the head monk's death—was easily endowed with riches and all the mendicant monks wore fine brocades.

The child went higher and higher into the forested mountains and, as if quite familiar with the terrain, walked straight to the Master Swordsman's hut. He walked in, stood before his host who happened to be meditating at the moment and, feeling unusually imperial after his solitary trip, demanded loudly, "Old Man, tell me your secrets! I shall one day become the greatest swordsman in all the Island Realm. Perhaps you will be fortunate enough to be my teacher."

He waited. Receiving no answer, he repeated his demand in a louder voice. He continued repeating it at intervals of two or three minutes for the greater part of an hour. Tiring at last, he sat and waited for all this very irritating religious stuff to come to an end.

At last, the Old Man cleared his throat, looked quietly at his guest and said, "Oh, Tai Kun, when those tiny, tiny peas between your thin little legs have grown large enough to be recognized as balls on a clear day, return and I shall make a superior flower-arranger of you."

Then the Old Man rose, gave the small rear a brief but memorable series of whacks and vanished into the forest with an ease that disdained speed.

He left behind a thoroughly enraged and adoring child. This was the first discipline that the young prince had ever received. It transmitted golden wisdom, respectfulness and a virile love far more satisfying than a father's dote or a mother's kiss.

Matriculation. . . .

The child took a quick tour of the hut kicking furiously at each of its sparse furnishings. His unseen attendants exchanged glances and made a note to offer the Old Man reparation in the event that he did not complain. The infant warrior then stomped out into the open, sat heavily in the little clearing and screamed as loudly as he could throughout the middle of the day.

This produced only dizziness, crimson in the face and thirst. Having proven himself more stubborn than most other animals under these circumstances, he gave up the screaming and sat in bitter reflection on great effort unrewarded. When he ran out of thoughts, he merely sat, for waiting is not a function of the intellect.

浪
人

After a short while of this, his attendants exchanged astonished glances. This had never happened before, but of course this had never been allowed to happen before. Adults are so chickenhearted when it comes to children. They, far more than their progeny, live in a terror of insecurity that they will not be loved.

The applicant continued to sit in the most precocious of patience as the afternoon melted away into evening, a tiny figure in a large clearing. His retinue conferred in whispers, debating every possible aspect of the situation. Their instructions having been to make themselves known only if needed, they resigned the cold mountain night to keeping watch and fitful sleep. City servants never like picnics.

The child, now coldly determined as a statue, keeled over and slept where he sat, much to the horror of his unseen court. He rose briefly to stretch at dawn, relieve himself in the bushes, drink at the spring and hasten back to his station. He was surprised to see the Old Man come out of the hut instead of the forest, urinate and again vanish among the trees of the forest.

The child's jaw muscles rippled as he debated whether to give this old shit another chance or not.

In whispers, his attendants debated whether they should come out and feed the undoubtedly hungry little warrior and thereby prolong this whole silly affair, or let him go hungry, cut it short himself and probably report to his uncle that he'd been criminally neglected.

As they paced anxiously backstage, the child sat all day glowering like Daruma and hardly moving except to shudder off flies. He gave no sign of being more hungry than determined. His guardians studied the little figure in awed silence then sent back to the Palace for instructions.

The Great Daimyo sent a brief message to the Old Swordsman indicating that he would exchange words with him concerning the child directly upon his arrival at the Palace. The answer was equally brief: "The son cannot learn respect when the father does not display it. I may not find time to talk to you after your arrival at my hut."

Early the next morning, the Lord and his immense retinue arrived at the mountain fastness. Thereafter the Great Man sat on the ground beside his precious heir and waited through the morning while the Old Man meditated.

Upon finishing, the Old Man came outside, sat before the two and bowed not too deeply. His behavior throughout this entire affair was that of a man fascinated with the Hereafter. He said, "You wish me to teach an art, which I have renounced, to a mere child who is prematurely haughty by at least eighty years. While he is a perfect type for hacking other fools to death with skill and equanimity, I am wholly unwilling to give such power into such hands for even so sanitary a purpose."

浪
人

The child, who had been maturing rapidly during the last twenty-four hours, bowed low and spoke: "No, Sensei, allow me to correct your understandable surmise. I wish to fight only one duel. After that, I shall give up my sword."

This strange information startled both men. The Uncle conjectured quite accurately and looked away, while the Old Swordsman, not yet aware of the domestic situation which had brought about this interview, looked directly at the child for the first time.

"You are willing to endure many, many years of training and hardship for just one duel? Surely you're a bit young to have been so magnificently wronged." He looked at the Daimyo who lowered his eyes, then back to the boy: "I assume it was not by a playmate but an adult, and that as you grow up, he also will mature. In which event, by the time you are a master swordsman, he will be as ancient as I am and your great duel will be against a man far past his prime, who will probably have forgotten his sin against you, if he ever knew it in the first place. Is this the victory you wish, *the death of a puzzled old man?*"

The child gritted his teeth at such a disturbing view of his heroic vendetta. It hadn't struck him that he would be fighting any but the young warrior in his prime who had stood on the landing that day or that the warrior would be so unsporting as to age while Vengeance was rushing through school to catch up with him.

The Old Swordsman remarked, "And I am invited to join in this long, this arduous and pious murder which I know nothing of. And, incidentally, what is to be my reward? Dancing girls? A golden prayer robe?"

The child bowed low again until his forehead kissed the earth and, with a fist beside each ear, destroyed the Old Man's scorn with these words: "But it is not certain that I'll win, Sensei! He is so great that I'm not sure I'll *want* to!"

The Old Man studied the child's back for a long while then smiled: "Sit up. Your face is dirty enough." He turned to the Lord: "I have no wish to pass on the art of this specific death, yet the wish for skill is rare and cannot be denied. If the child stays here with me, I do not promise to make a swordsman of him, a tea master or even a good woodgatherer. Perhaps a man but nothing else. But it will be in my own time, in my own way and without a breath of interference coming up from the Plain. And one other stipulation more important than the rest. There must never be an effort made to reward me in any way, no gold, good words nor favors of any hue. For I accept this task not for him nor you but for myself. I have a fool's need to win where once I triply lost."

The Old Man knew. Had the Daimyo any doubt

浪
人

before that this was merely grave impudence instead of utter superiority, it was now gone. He astonished everyone by now bowing low. He restrained himself from bidding the child farewell in so austere an atmosphere and departed blushing faintly at the length of his cortege. He was halfway back to the Palace on the Plain before realizing that this whole momentous interchange had taken place without a single word from him himself.

It had been a solemn pact solely between a sixty-year-old recluse and a thin little boy of nine.

The jackass who is my teacher. . . .

For the first year, the boy chopped wood.

The initial month shot past and he obeyed with the docility of eager anticipation. He even took a little pride in learning to wield the ax. Sensei's edict that the fire should be kept burning night and day seemed a little eccentric to the boy, but it was all part of the game of Getting There. He even came to remotely enjoy the need to rouse every hour or so through the night to toss on more wood. Very soon he could tell from the sound of the crackle whether the fire needed fuel—even with his eyes shut. His sleep was closer to the surface now and his waking more instant, his skill as a lackey matured as Keeper of the Flame.

During the second thirty days, he frowned now and again, and picked his callouses petulantly. Each night he told himself that surely tomorrow the actual lessons would begin. There followed uninterrupted weeks of mere chopping and rising rage. He played defiant little games with the wood, learning to chop it with increasing ease from a variety of absurd positions. And it became apparent to him that he had made a mistake in the choice of teachers.

At the end of the third month, he was saying just one more day of this foolishness and he'd throw the ax into the Hanging Lake, go home to his uncle with the whole story and *then* certain people would find out who was running this province. Of course, he really should give the Old Man a chance first, perhaps have a candid talk with him and find out when the studies would begin and what to expect by way of progress.

To this end, he brushed a short, formal note and slipped it halfway under the Old Man's door so he'd know when it had been picked up from inside. It remained there an hour. Then another, then days and weeks, and soon he noticed it wasn't so white anymore after much weather and many glances. His irritation grew by the day and he rehearsed all sorts

浪
人

of deadly remarks clearly to show how he'd been wronged. Finally deciding to withdraw his kindly offered opportunity for the Old Man to explain himself, he snatched the note from under the door and went straight to the fire with it. Opening it up so it would burn faster, he discovered that the sheet was blank. This wasn't his note; it wasn't even folded the same. He'd been furious about the wrong thing all this time!

This doubled his anger at Sensei. On top of not replying to a perfectly civil request, he had to play this low little trick on the most eager student *he'd* ever have. What a mean old stinker! And he'd begged to come here!

He should leave right now. It might look to some as if he were giving up, and he'd be secretly smiled at by the entire Palace, but he'd show them all he could learn the Sword elsewhere without all this waste of time. Of course, he could see the Old Man laughing to himself at the loss of his only student. And the smug old bastard would think himself quite justified in having made that outrageous remark about flower-arranging right in front of everyone. And he'd laugh uproariously at having put just *two* on top of the boy's mound of rice each time they had peas for supper. It was too much to bear. Or it would have been if a samurai did not always keep in mind that *to bear what you think you cannot bear is really to bear.*

So it is that great thoughts help us through our smaller crises.

In the fourth month, he took courage in his two hands, leaped before the Old Man, bowed and respectfully inquired as to the date of his first lesson in *kendo*. The voice above him murmured, "Hm, the carp that yearns for a worm cannot be enjoying his diet of flies." The boy mulled this remark over for several days sure that it had some deep meaning. He finally came to the conclusion that it was neither meaningful, nor deep nor an answer. He again knelt and asked his question. This time the answer was, "When you are ready." To which the boy exclaimed, "I'm ready now!" at which the Old Man rejoined, "So? Drop your pants and let's take a look."

Wanting to howl with rage, the boy returned to his ax and block, and splintered log after log after log. And thereafter, each night by the fire, carefully examined his male parts for signs of burgeoning.

He saw none and he despaired as time and the world rushed by. Added to his chopping was a new water chore. Seven times a day he must carry two brimming buckets up the steep mountain path so that the Old Man could bathe there at the hut. This meant that he must chop wood faster for he now had the same amount to do in half the former time.

Additional outrages appeared. He must now read and write and memorize morning and night, in

浪
人

spite of the universally known fact that all true samurai scorn the scholastic. But the longer he took to learn, the less time he had for the mandatory water and the mandatory wood. At first, he often labored far into the night, slept restlessly and was kicked awake like an Eta for letting the fire go out. No longer did he watch butterflies like other little boys, play hiding games and lie looking for animals in the clouds. There was time for nothing but unremitting work to which he applied himself as if afraid of losing his job. And he was. It would have given the Old Man too much pleasure.

And so it was that he gradually discovered that all interest in life had left him. Nothing sparked his interest in this sterile void. He missed not butterflies nor games nor clouds; they were things gone in a vanished childhood that he could hardly recollect. With them went sudden joys and rage, all spark, all smiles, even impatience and the treasure of his hate. He seemed reduced to a flat, dull simmer in which even the two green vegetable spheres upon his rice did not rouse him. Crushed as the peasants he'd heard about, his life was a steady, heartless moving with no more purpose than simply keeping things as they were from getting worse.

When the first year had passed, he had not even the interest to spit in the Old Man's face much less avenge his Father and his Mother. He was nothing but tired, inside and out. And when the last shred of meaning left all this monotony, he sighed and decided to leave on the night of the next full moon. It would be pleasant to walk away through the glowing forest. This lunar choice naturally indicated whole universes of joy still remaining in his sturdy little frame. He may have felt like an old man at the age of ten, scorned the giggling boys his age who sometimes passed the hut on outings, and forgiven Sensei his wrinkles, but he was still boy enough to count the pleasures that he now declined.

He didn't take the walk through his moonlit forest. Something happened that made him entirely forget it.

And it hurt.

Four feet of bamboo. . . .

He was carrying the last of two brimming buckets up the mountain path. The blow came from behind and landed squarely across his right ear. The tremendous pain was like looking into the sun. He blinked and found himself on the ground. The buckets were rolling happily back down the mountain and the Old Man was looking down at him

浪
人

with great satisfaction as if he'd wanted to do this cruel thing for a long, long time. He was leaning on a length of new bamboo, apparently cut just for this occasion.

It hurt badly but the worst part was the boy's helplessness to stop a few renegade tears. He wiped them away as if they were dirt and knelt to explain why he was so late in bringing the last of the water. But he'd hardly begun before the Old Man said, "Who cares about bath water! It only gets dirty and has to be thrown out!" and walked away leaving the boy nonplussed.

Frowning, the boy rose and started back down for the buckets. He'd hardly gone three steps before the bamboo struck again. It roared across his shoulders with shocking pain. The boy let out a howl and scrambled as fast as he could on hands and knees into the bushes. He peered back out. The Old Man was looking at him intently. The boy gasped as he realized that the old bastard had finally gone completely mad. He hadn't any idea what to do so he just crouched there and looked back intently.

He remained hiding long after the madman had gone into the hut and slid the door shut. While trying to decide a course of action, the boy crept carefully down the hill, automatically found and filled the buckets, and brought them back up. He was just emptying the first into the bath barrel when something told him to duck. As a consequence the third blow glanced off his shoulder. He fled around a corner of the hut. Peering back, he found the clearing empty. The old coot was fast. There was the faintest rustle behind him. Without waiting to look, the boy leaped forward, but not soon enough to escape an exquisite rap on the coccyx. Clutching his little tail, he fled moaning into the forest.

There were three more attacks before supper. By then, the boy was so jumpy that he decided against eating. Ordered to come in, however, he obeyed. The old hands held out his full bowl abruptly and he jumped away, blushed and returned. The old voice said, "Fool, even mad old teachers don't waste good food."

They ate in their usual silence then the Old Man said to him through the twilight, "An animal will jump at every sound, a leaf in the wind, a falling cone. A disciplined man will move only when it is necessary." There was a ruminative pause then the addendum: "The moment *before* it is necessary."

The rare words did not comfort the boy. Senility is sickness to the young, and suspect. He studied the wrinkled monster with one eye and went slowly around corners until bedtime. Then he found himself reluctant to sleep in the light of the fire. He pulled his mat into a dark corner and only dozed between fire-feedings. Twice he heard something unusual in the night and woke standing up.

It wasn't for many, many nerve-wracked days that the boy remembered his decision about the journey in the full moon. He smiled bitterly, re-

浪
人

membering that he had been crushed by monotony back then. Sweet monotony! Now, flinching at every leaf in the wind and every fallen cone, he yearned for just a few minutes of comfortable, restful monotony.

Thereafter, he never turned his back on the Old Man again. He might be carrying a load of wood, reading a sutra or helpless in the bathing barrel, but part of his mind was always alert for that vicious stick of bamboo. When it came, he let fly what he carried, dived for cover and cleaned up the mess later when the Fiend was gone.

Yet in time he found it possible to duck instead of dive, to veer and not drop the wood, the water or the book. He was almost surprised to find it was possible to move with caution and still get all of his chores done in good time. The unwarranted persecution was only as much of an obstacle as his lack of skill allowed it to be.

And in time he counted fewer bruises and nursed fewer aches. This told him, with sober pride, that the bamboo stick wasn't connecting so often. This gave him a grain of pride and, without knowing it, the pride allowed him to discard a grain of fear. Eventually he realized wordlessly that there is a great difference between the self-contained alertness of a man and that lip of panic on which a wild thing lives and wastes itself. But only a fool loses fear consciously, and the boy remained safe in unanalyzed growth.

It became a grave game in which he gradually forgot to be angry with his teacher. When the bamboo fell with unexpected ingenuity and landed full and hard, his first thought was in admiration: *I am proud of my adversary.* Then no longer did he merely pass through a door thinking of something else. It became an act of dangerous importance. Nor did he round a corner unthinkingly, approach the top of a hill blithely, nor pass closely by a tree. Reverie was replaced by exquisite attention to what he was doing. Each act called for total concentration if he was to avoid pain, a fall of pride and the tattoo of a bruise. So, to avoid hurt, he learned to perceive Everything that is Now.

Later, there were times when he came to sense that which he could not perceive. He stood long minutes outside the dark door somehow certain that there was a raised and waiting stick within. He stood motionless for two then three, five then ten minutes, and at last realizing he was a fool to hesitate all night outside an empty room, shrugged, entered and fell beneath an outraged blow that repeated itself with mounting fury as the old voice grated, "You knew, you knew, and yet you used *this* door! Damn you, at least *try* to keep me interested in holding school!"

So he walked more softly and he broke up the patterns of shortness, ease and opportunity that are deadly habit. If the stick waited at some turning that he always took, he changed the route and went some

浪
人

longer, less expected way. Time was not important. And he learned to still his humming as he moved about his chores. There was no need to sing when his spirits rose, no need to make himself known to the forest world. The vanity of carving his name in air gave way to the pleasure of unwatched watching.

Unknown to him, the boy became quieter within as well. Concentration does not permit of fancies and debates, poetries and orations in one's inner auditorium when the stick might fall at any time. He stilled his quarrelsome mind so that he could hear the world outside, and he deeply liked the things he heard. *Not my song, but yours.*

His second year ended with a triumph that was too incredible to believe. Walking silently, he came upon his teacher waiting for him faced the other way! There was hardly an instant of joy before he fell into a terrible concern for the Old Man's skill! The poor man stood helpless! And further, how desperately humiliating to have so poor a student catch one in an awkwardness!

Silent as a shadow, he went back the way he came. The Old Man turned in time to see him go. His old eyes went wide then melted into a smile.

The next day he sat in the center of the clearing and summoned the boy from his work. The student knelt, bowed and sat straight before him. Their eyes met and held, and they exchanged many kinds of silent information. Then the Old Man held out to him a bamboo stick of his own, a new one cut for this occasion.

With the greatest effort, the boy reached out slowly and took the stick, slowly bowed and slowly rose to walk down the forest path in dignity.

The Old Man had only to glance at that young back to know the boy was crying quiet, sober tears.

The interruption. . . .

Each attainment brings its own despair. No ruler could have taken more pride in his scepter than the boy in his bamboo stick—and the Old Man flicked it from his hands with derisive ease. The boy picked it up, took his stance and somehow there it went again. He picked it up with absolute determination, gritted his teeth and gripped it until his knuckles were white. It flew from his hands as if escaping. He picked up the bamboo stick a thousand times until his heart knew he could never be a swordsman. The skill was beyond him. The only question was how 浪 to leave most unobtrusively. 人

But life on the mountain was intensely interesting. *109*

With no set practice periods, the boy carried the stick under his belt as a permanent part of his clothing and merely dropped what he was doing when attacked. Each duel lasted until both of them were sure that he'd been killed yet once again. The question was not whether but when. Holding the stick with an iron grip and wary as a hummingbird, he faced his impassive adversary knowing that the only possible victory lay in retaining his weapon a moment longer than he had last time. He did battle for each second separately and counted them like coins before he went to sleep.

Yet, for the thousand and first time, there the stick lay upon the ground. It was maddening. It was unbelievable. It was a magic and he wanted to cry out to the too superior man, "Damn you, at least give me a *chance!*" until remembering the eleven gracious teachers at the Palace who refused him skill by letting him win each match.

He happened to notice that the thumb of Sensei's upper hand curled slightly down just before each lunge. The boy began to watch it intently and to avoid the deadly whir once or twice in ten. He thought, "At last, I'm beginning to learn something," and was a breath away from pride, when the Old Man followed his gaze, frowned and curled his thumb without a lunge. The boy dodged instantly. The Old Man grunted in disgust and walked away without bothering to kill him.

That remained a puzzle to him for many days

and he searched Sensei closely for other little quirks. Then his own voice said to him, "How often would a swordsman fight the same man and learn his little ways? With cold steel, each man once." And with infinite slowness, he learned the precise place to study in an adversary. The clue for action lay in the eyes but not in any move they made. One immersed oneself in the eyes in order to *become* the adversary. All else followed.

It was in the fifth month of the bamboo stick that he finally made a thrust of his own. Wholly unpremeditated, it was a wide miss and followed by a knuckle-cracking blow, but it had happened at last. Sensci stood looking at him a long moment, nodded and walked off. It was a proud day in the hut.

Not quite a year later, the boy parried a blow and brought his stick down on the Old Man's shoulder with accuracy and force. He instantly dropped the weapon and knelt to ask forgiveness when he found himself hugged firmly in two strong old arms. And the old voice whispered in the carefully awkward sentimentality of a warrior that is *bushi no nasake,* "I shall not forget this blow."

A moment later the boy was scrambling madly for his stick under a storm of blows that echoed about the clearing.

Another year passed and he became a most mature thirteen.

There was jubilation in the Palace when a messenger returned with the news that the "young man" was ready to get the feel of a real sword. The Daimyo and his counselors debated for days whether the blade should be the Sukesada in the Great Hall or the Yoshimitsu being cared for by a cousin. A whole procession brought the chosen weapon up the mountain. The uncle was last to recognize the strong young man with the tightly bound topknot who met him with grave courtesy. The presentation ceremony waited on the teacher who didn't come out of the forest until it was almost begun without him. He stood at the edge of the clearing and demanded in a loud, clear voice, "Are you elated that he has come this much nearer death? Go home and we will study the sword to see if it is really his."

The higher counselors were irritated at this arrogance. But the Daimyo said, "Only one man has cause to complain. I will listen to him when he speaks." They left without further talk.

The youth wasn't sure he liked the sword, though to the eye it was a jewel. It seemed so light after his familiar bamboo stick. The Old Man took it into the clearing and slashed the air for most of an hour; he handed it back in silence. The young man also tried it on the air, tried it every day alone—for one does not practice steel upon another man. His *kiai* echoed through the forest in the morning mist, at midday and twilight when the rice-steam writhed to him like the ghost of a serpent upon the air.

He never knew when the testing ended. He was

simply aware one day that the sword was really his, part of him and wholly right. And that it had been for a long, long time, perhaps even before the procession up the path, and that it would always be no matter who might own it next. It never again left his side. Nor did he ever tell a soul the name he had given it, a name so secret that his lips had never formed it.

A batch of days came in which he was plagued by a sense of having forgotten one of his chores. In was neither the wood nor the water, and he'd done all of his duties of practice and meditation, bathing and study, yet there remained this trifle nibbling at the back of his mind. Not until weeks later did he remember that his fourteenth birthday had come and gone.

He remembered the tale of the great siege of Osaka and the young son of Ieyasu who wept at being placed in the rear of the army. When an old counselor consoled him with reminders of the long life of heroic deeds ahead, Ieyasu's son fixed him with an indignant glare and said, *"Can ever my fourteenth year come round again?"*

The boy took a deep breath and went about his duties.

Now their bouts with wooden swords took on a fury that stilled the forest about them, and the young man carefully crippled his skill so as not to hurt Sensei. At length, the Old Man said, "At this point, you have as much to learn from meditation 浪 人

as you have from me. Go especially to the Shinto shrine on the dark side of the Mountain." He went that same day and found the room empty of everything but a mirror in the gloom.

He found it odd, then acceptable, then finely pertinent.

Now, he chopped wood and swept the floor and fetched water, all with the supreme care of reverence. The months passed a moment at a time and each instant was a golden awareness of itself. There was neither past nor future. Purpose and determination faded into mere sounds, and as he climbed out of the bathing barrel, the Old Man brought his stick lightly up between the wet young legs and said, "What happened to the peas? You've turned them into acorns. Stop before they're pine cones. Pride is a burden."

The young man blushed and smiled and went about his work, his study, his practice and his growth. He became fifteen—and a man.

He was never aware of the season, the day nor hour in which he became the greatest swordsman in all the Island Realm. Shielded from this deadly knowledge by his desperate efforts to *miss* his treasured adversary, the thought never entered his mind that he was anything but a student.

Then one day, gathering firewood, he came to a cliff looking down upon the Hanging Lake. There he saw a man and a woman in a little covered boat that made an arrow of its wake. He was stunned beyond comprehension. He woke from a long, sweet sleep into cacophony, assuming that pain is more real than pleasure.

An hour later he was gone, leaving this note behind: "My parents made me a child. My teacher made me a man." There was a long, thoughtful space then these words: *"Nor does the severed limb cease to be part of the Tree."*

The Old Man read it, carefully folded the paper and placed it upon the fire. Then he laid his bamboo practice stick upon the flames, watched it burn and rose to finish what he'd been doing the day the child arrived.

浪
人

The journey through Hell with a torch. . . .

On high wooden clogs, the Young Samurai began his strange journey.

He strode the Great Highway for eight days pausing briefly to nap and lunch, for which he paid with the coins he had taken up the Mountain as a child. On the ninth day, he stopped abruptly and looked upon a long-forgotten tree. A shimmer of joyful terror ran through him at the sight, for time is smashed by the properties of childhood and we have no certain age. Walking more slowly with each step, he went forward to the Palace of his birth.

First, he noticed the immense silence. This great house had been a place which never slept. Now he saw Fertility's other self, Decay, at its noiseless, unseen work grinding all his babyhood to dust and smoke and finally to dreams of vast inaccuracy.

The wind rattled loose boards which never would have been allowed in his father's day, and wary little wild things were lords and landlords of the silent realm where their great-great-grandfathers, diminutive generations ago, had once risked death for crumbs. Now their descendants avenged them by being unaware of all this vanished splendor.

In an excitement of expectancy which he could not understand, the young man moved toward his childhood rooms in the Pepper Court. He stood where he had slept and saw again what had happened over there, and there and here and just outside the door. Then, with a jolt, he realized that this was not his room at all, but some cousin's, and that he'd remembered North outside the wrong wall all these years.

He swallowed hard as he discovered: *Then there is nothing here.*

The absolute certainty that he had left a mark was just an illusion of his species. The laughter and the tears were not monumental stuff. Soon the Forest would follow the wary little things and "home" would become a vague Somewhere Over There among the trees, or maybe just "over there." And shortly after that, the question would arise of which forest it had been.

He understood as little of the great sadness of Going as he had the excitement of Coming Home. Being still a boy, he felt that it should be obverse.

The grown boy's private thunder returned as he

浪
人

stood at the rear entrance and looked down at the remaining sticks of the Landing at the river's edge. The Great Day was still not over. He heard shouts and screams, and looked upon a brilliance that made him squint. He hurried down the memories of a path and looked out on the powerful stream. It was smaller though it hadn't shrunk.

He turned his back on the Palace and the Landing, and began to move along the shore in the direction that the little covered boat had gone. It seemed to be just beyond each bend. He moved in nervous expectation.

A steady sound droned ahead. At each bend, it became a sharp degree louder as at the opening of a door. Suddenly he stood in a maelstrom of sound and stared into the rapids. He saw the whiteness of death and knew the little boat could not have gone beyond this point.

The white roaring meant another thing as well. This journey, the years of study, bruised despair and hoarded hate—even the Vow itself—had all been waste from the moment the helpless boat came around that bend so many, many years ago. Far from a high-minded hero, he'd been dedicated to Nothing, the dupe of an assumption and in grim pursuit of the moveless dead.

Most would-be saints have a prior destiny with Waste.

Eight years of weariness came running up. In sudden weakness, he sat as if to never rise again.

Only when the Sun impaled Herself on trees did he pull himself away from the white roar as from addiction.

There was a village on the Highway just beyond the sound of the river. He took a dreary little room and sat through the darkness of the night contemplating the panorama of his waste. With morning came steaming tea and the thought of broken bodies on the rocks. He asked the innkeeper about his dead. The man insisted that he knew nothing whatsoever of the pair. His positiveness was a pathetic revelation of the lie, which largely concerned the fact that his second cousin on his mother's side now owned the Ronin's Pecker Two and kept it hidden in cloth underneath his floor. Useless and unused.

The young man went on to the next village south. Over rice, he asked this second innkeeper about the two who must have died in the rapids. At the reply, his attention roared in a delirium of intentness.

"A great samurai and a beautiful lady? Oh yes, they passed this way. But that was many, many years ago. Wet and without sandals, hungry and without coin. For some reason, he hid his sword in the bushes at the edge of the village. But everyone—all of us—treated them quite well, fed them, roomed them and even gave them shoes. Believe me, this is true. And in return, the samurai robbed the little 浪 bachelor in the last house down the road of all the 人 pennies he'd saved from boy to man. He's dead now, the kindly little fool, long dead and on some certain nights you can plainly hear the jingling of pennies on the wind that flows through his empty house. He left no sons."

The innkeeper paused and looked out to the Highway: "And she was so beautiful, fragile as a flower and just as helpless. Yes, yes."

The words whipped the young man's heart back to mighty purpose. His Mission rose to him directly from the dead and he left the inn with great determination.

No more debilitating doubts.

At the third village he began to hear of a most unusual pair of beggars. She was a great lady, as the wise could quickly see, though there were those who called her madam and him pimp, and turned them out. But *we* knew at once she was not accustomed to the degradation of the Road and gave her all we could and tended her as well as any starving farmer can. It was sad to see her go. But he was fierce as any beast and stole, mauled and slashed any in his way. One died. She scolded him like an empress and he looked away saying nothing.

They watched the young man go on to the next village and whispered nervous speculations.

He walked in rising anger. How could he have stayed secluded on the mountain for so many lulling years! What was any monastery but a gelding of the eyes, as if Wrong ceases to exist if it isn't seen!

Each successive village had a little batch of incidents that made him sick with fury. And they told him eagerly what he seemed to want to hear, adding something here and there. The young man felt guilt at opening old wounds and wondered at the relish with which the stories tumbled out. They seemed to cherish these old sorrows and welcome the chance to cry again old tears, complain in mounting tones of the long forgotten woe and shake the fist again at the point on the plain where the road vanished.

They appeared eager to rouse his anger at the ancient crimes as if thinking his "justice" would bring restitution. None seemed to know that justice never rights a wrong but only extends the pain to at least one more.

Feeling a great burden, he listened and wondered from their cries, what they expected beyond the criminal's death. Surely they didn't expect him to see the Beast tucked safely into Hell as well. Nor did it seem that Hell would be enough, for long after the Ronin was dust with dust these weeping little folk would go on beating with their aching fists the stone of irreparable loss which is part of the House of Life.

So he took on their griefs to feed his own, used borrowed tears to affirm his resolution and walked on with his Vow as strong as the day he'd watched the Battle of the Landing with wonder and with hate.

浪
人

The visiting hour for prisoners. . . .

Slowly but surely, there was born in the young samurai a secret grief that made his hate of the Beast soar up to the faintest star, and each village made it a greater agony of shame. For, as he listened to the thousand versions of the beggars' passing, he was forced to realize that his gentle Mother was no captive.

Her part of the Grand Adventure became more dominant with each account. Now he understood why they'd looked at him in such stymied silence when he told them he was her avenging son. And why their replies stumbled over hyphens and made the abductor a Beast of Beasts. Later, when he did not name himself, they spoke freely of this woman's shameless begging, prostitution and coin acumen.

The young man forgave and discounted their exaggerations which rose from vague hopes of reparation as if they were unaware that even the most cautious understatement could not veil the crimes that had been visited upon them by the

Ronin. An extremely generous apology for the Beast by the patriarch of a great new monastery—built by the anonymous gift of three rubies—did not obscure this trail of wanton cruelty.

Yet, as the villages ahead parted and passed on either side of him, she appeared more and more surely the instigator and the man only the executioner of her crimes.

The worst of these was meanness. She grasped every penny, bargained violently over every price, ate leftovers, patched her clothes badly and slept in stables, when she could have had the poor mild best with her earnings as an accomplished whore. In matters of money, her eyes went wide and her voice shrill, and she would sink to any necessary depth to come away with the coin of a successful bargain.

This was his Mother, the great and gentle Lady of the Palace, the dream that made his childhood significant and sweet. His throat ached to scream his fury at the man who had so changed her elemental goodness!

It was early morning. The rain was fine as hair and steady as an executioner's drum. Methodically placing one foot before the other, he approached the house where he'd been told she stayed. It was on the west side of the village where the lower classes are, where Eta live and executions take place. The house was an unrepaired and dirty place with refuse thrown out any door; inside were the quarreling, small-town geisha who hated rising early to do servants' chores.

They watched the door slide open and each stopped where she was to look at him. Before his air of virgin virility, they could neither move nor speak. Then an older woman came forward pushing them aside and scolding them for manners that they did not have. Seeing the youth, she curdled into smiles and simperings, led him into her best room and clapped imperiously for many little services.

He knew her instantly but had to search for familiar features. The woman sitting on the other side of the quilt-covered *kotatsu* wore a thick coat of rice-powder on face and chin. The contrast of unhealthy white with her weather-darkened neck was as painful as smelling the fact that a princess has not bathed yet chatters with the assurance of a blossom. There were bloodshot eyes that cosmetics could accent but never hide, and the wrinkled ghosts of two once lovely hands.

He could not say, "I am your son." The sight of her face would be more than he was man enough to bear. Yet he did not lie, for a samurai has no need to lie. He simply told his mission and asked if she had seen the pair. She stared at him with tilted head and fixed smile until near the end, then abruptly clapped her hands, called for hotter tea and apologized for both service and her interruption—patting her hair carefully. From then on, she fixed many folds in her robe, said *Ah!* many times, stirred the coals under the blanket and patted and patted her hair again.

When he had finished, she ran a tongue over dry lips and said yes indeed it just so happened that she knew them well. They had passed this way and the Lady had, in this very town, finally escaped her abductor. Her eyes hopped about the room as she spoke as if to follow her racing thoughts. His mother was—at this very moment—recovering in a mountain place not many *ri* from here. But he must not see her at this time so delicate was her condition. Perhaps on his way back from The Mission she would be able to see him. Yes, *then!* And what a beautiful reunion that would be!

He asked how long she'd been here and the woman shrugged as if the time were not important: "Oh, perhaps a year, a little more or less. But, mind you, she's been through a terrible ordeal. She is ill and weary beyond all imagination." She searched his face as if looking for one line of doubt. He returned her gaze with a still face, nodded and said *Yes* many times.

Feeling herself believed, she tumbled into a long tale of the Lady's myriad misfortunes. Her voice was carried along on a whining singsong flow such as village wives use and never guess. She told each step of the Journey that he knew so well, lied where he knew the truth, and each lie made larger and more necessary the next. The words came out in one long and uncontrolled gush, that made his gaze keep falling to the floor.

浪
人

And when every desperate detail was told, she sat in wordless nonplus, stripped naked by the tale that she herself had told. For, whatever her misfortune, the black fact remained that here she sat now in this house. Here, here, and nowhere else but here for perhaps a year, a little more, a little less. Nothing in the universe could explain that.

Seeing the inexplicable, she blurted out with passion, "I know that he's been gone a year, but he swore to kill her if she didn't wait for him! And, if you knew the Beast, you'd know he would. So she waited, stayed and waited, and each day told herself *Perhaps tomorrow*. And the days became months and she waited faithfully. It seemed beyond belief that he could leave her *after all she'd done for him*."

She stopped abruptly as if hearing the words from someone else, as if hearing their terrible confession that could not be taken back. Then, with real tears, she crawled to him, clutched his waist and cried, *"You must kill him, kill him, kill him!"*

The young man sat in embarrassment until her tears were used, waited until she wiped the ruinous rivulets channeling her powdered face and avoided her desperate eyes made redder by weeping.

She held him and looked up: "When you come back, she'll be well and lovely as she ever was. And you and she can go somewhere and live, you two. How proud she'll be of such a son, and what a mother she will be! Like none before! And she's not poor, you know. She took with her a bag of rubies—" Here her desperate hands felt her belt, rubbed it, pressed it, smoothed it. "Fortune enough to buy you everything you've ever wished. For she's sold not one single stone but left them all intact, a heritage for you. She's not so much as looked at them for years, because they're yours and will wait for your return. But come back quickly, find him, avenge her honor—and your father's life—and hurry back. Because she can't abide this low and vile and filthy life. Oh, come back for her as soon as his blood is fresh upon the ground! Promise me!"

He nodded. When she insisted many times, he said, with an astonished heart, "I promise."

Then he quickly rose, took his leave and walked out into the street and down away to some unseen place where he could vomit out his heart.

Chaos and the painted tree. . . .

The Young Man had once heard one of his pompous teachers say, "It is clear that all men house a Devil, Saint and Fool. Even more obscure is the Ultimate Sin in nurturing any one of these in another."

Selecting the part of this congenial to his understanding, the Youth chose the sickness of hating the Beast who had so unstintingly helped his sainted Mother to become both fool and devil. However willing she might have been to learn and however incidental that it had by chance fallen to this one man and not another of the billion nurturers on the earth, he set about to study Hate and wear it as a precious jewel.

Then it can be seen that inner events were approaching the point where mere perseverance must join revenge as the motive of his search. Indeed, he repeated his Vow like a sutra to drown out the fact that he had started life the envy of all men in having a Mission so Righteous, so Noble and so Good that no man of rectitude would have refused to undertake it.

Now, things were not so clear.

While still in his Mother's village, he began to hear confusing tales of the Beast's departure. They said he'd had some drunken fit, a stroke of midnight madness, and that he'd fled into the night without his Sword. No one inquired where. It was enough that he was gone, taking no road but an arrow-straight flight across the Plain.

The Youth could not believe that he had left his Soul behind until he held it in his hands. It was extremely precious and a thing of great beauty. All who beheld it said a long and whispered *Ahhhhhhh* at the strip of silver steel made with love and skill for the single purpose of opening live human flesh.

The fact that the Beast might have undergone some moral change in no way altered the need of Justice. He might now see quite clearly what he'd been and what he'd done; he might even have entered some passing phase of star-shattering repentance and revel grandly in self-hate. But he himself would be the first to see that Justice is concerned with but one act and that a crime, and all crime must be avenged. No good can wipe it out, for if sins can be erased by mortal men themselves, then all social structures fall and the world is made ruin by a chaos of brotherhood.

The youth repeated endlessly, "Repentance will not do!" as if confronted with a threat. The thought of the Beast repentant added despising to his hate, for what is more revolting than a villain without the courage of his convictions? Marked for destruction, a man can yet be respected as long as he swaggers and shouts defiance of all laws of gods and men.

But the humbled criminal stains the executioner's sword and sours Justice at its peak. He demonstrates for all time that Justice cannot relent without vanishing and transforming the noble Sword into a swatter of flies. He takes the meaning from our own goodness, makes waste our outrage, reduces Law to babble and forces us to justify the Vow that cannot be explained: *Oh, you Gods, give us villains that we are proud to kill!*

浪
人

129

Carrying all this worded tumult like a tub of adders, the young man repeated *"Mother!"* endlessly and traced the empty shell of a former monster to a crossroad in the Plain. Following the echoes of a walking dead man devoid of top-knot, sword and love and hope, he came to the place of the steaming tea, stopped and looked about, and sat in the shade of a tree with leaves that did not move. It was painted on the sky.

Morning died. The earth listed and made afternoon, and he sat biting fingernails until they bled. At last he sighed and sat up straight, closed his eyes and studied the Mirror in the Shrine. He stayed within until he was ready to admit that this Journey had no higher purpose than the extermination of a dog. The monumental admission came without great thunder in the sky. There was one small shimmer of the leaves then they returned to paint.

He rose with a sign and a purpose that had the single merit of being better than none.

The Young Warrior entered the last village. It had no name and it was indeed bewitched. Free from the melancholy of all the other clusters on the road, this village had people who seemed to actually understand the *Bushido* credo: *Live when it is right to live, and die when it is right to die.* Apparently aware that Heaven's at the heart of Hell, they told quite casually of the Old Halved Monk, the girl with the rabbit tail, the three young boys standing naked and astonished in the stream and, worst of all, the

Shopkeeper who lost two fingers then a hand—and lived.

Outraged, the Young Warrior threw back his head and laughed, and they laughed with him, though a bit uncertainly. Oh, the black delight! What joy to know the Villain was really worth the Vow, the Journey worth the Steps, and to see all things again in only black and white! No more thrall of color wherein there is no choice! The Beast was again guilty of immortal outrage and he was damned and he must die by the blade of this virgin Sword! Let him weep, pray and promise, do any penance this side of death, let him even bow and murmur *Yes* to what must be, and he would still die by the fury of *this* dedication! There was no more escape for him, for the Young Knight of the Vow had come to an end of thinking. If *to know and act are one,* then the Beast was already rotting in the Sun!

They pointed, and with tremendous zest he set out for the Black Mountain and the place called *Lip of Hell.* Here the quest that had begun in baby-hood in sight of the Landing would end and he would at last be a man.

浪
人

A navel for the Gut of Wrath. . . .

A man conscious of being in some way great does not give gifts. He rids himself of excess. For this reason, he always scorns appreciation.

The Ronin had never given anything away that he himself needed. Now, when he *must* give to save his very soul, he found giving a complex art, intricate with motive and rife with fatal credit. Like the great black bear that the Ainu worship, he bumbled about in blunt generosities and groaned that he had not the fingers to perform this delicate task.

First, it took him eons of awkwardness to discover that all gifts are not welcome, that a show of gratitude is not mandatory nor desired by the best of givers, that contests of reciprocity are a bestial travesty on man, and that the sweet or deadly reason for giving is more important than the gift.

From his extreme humility, everyone at once sensed that here was a sinner desperately afraid of Hell and using them as a bribe to slip into the suburbs of Heaven. They knew him to be impersonal and overeager, and received his fumbling kindnesses with the blank eyes of the damned.

Wholly ignorant of living in community, he failed completely as an unpaid public servant. He was confronted with the escape of monastic life, but rightly feared that it would be too self-revealing. So he stumbled on, trying to find a way to Give Himself in a world where such needs are at best a little silly, quite suspect and perhaps a little mad.

And he was a little mad, for such madness is the earmark of true sanity and must be sealed away from all analysis.

Alone in a shrine, he knelt before a slightly smiling wooden thing and said, "I do not understand. As a killer, I felt far more accepted. You must tell me how to make myself wanted, needed, valued! What can I do to live *in* the world and not forever on the edges!" It went on smiling slightly and he went on begging as if wood had lungs. At last the two of them reached an impasse where the smile could only broaden almost to a laugh and the suppliant rise in rage.

"So even you won't have me!" He walked to the door and turned: "But I'm not deceived! You do not answer because you do not know! Ha? Well, I'll find the answer for myself and let *you* know. 浪人 *133*

I'll make an answer if I have to, and you'll end up knocking at my door and begging to come in. You'll learn from me that gods have no use except to serve!" His feet thudded across the porch as he went.

The wooden smile was not quite so sure when he had gone.

He began to walk and then to climb. Perhaps things would be different on the other side of the Mountain. The path grew narrow among the crags and at last thinned to a tiny ledge, an almost unseen scar across the precipice with only mist below. Huddled here on the last open space were several frightened travelers. They watched with open mouths as a young man edged his way with burdens on his back and trembling hands searching for a hold. Moving a step at a time and frozen by the wind, he slowed and slowed and finally stopped unable to go on or back.

Without a thought of watching gods, the Ronin pushed the travelers back and slid along the path hardly wider than his feet. Alarmed, the wind whipped at his hair and clothes. The Mountain stared. The rock wall was smooth under his searching hands, the ledge a mockery, the goal but mist. Tense as a *koto* string stretched to its ultimate, he moved in the slow haste of a man possessed.

The self-trapped man ahead sank slowly to one knee. The Ronin, feeling little sections crumble beneath his weight, hurried on, one inch and then another. The young man sat and clung and stared down into the mist. With wind that drowned out sound and a burden on his back past which he could not see, he didn't know that someone had come to join him in his death until a great hand closed around his arm.

Startled, he turned to see, and slipped off into the void. The Ronin, pressing against the cliff, held on. The young man and his burden dangled in the air. The deep voice said, "Don't try to save yourself or you'll kill us both. Just hang. Don't try to move."

Hanging helpless, the young man laughed in terror and obeyed by fainting.

The Ronin turned. His face against the cliff, one hand clutching the rock ahead and the other holding the limp form of a total stranger behind him, he started back in one more experiment with death.

As minute followed minute and the travelers stared and the Mountain blew the wind to ice, he slid one foot on and the other after. Sweat soaked his body and his breath was gasps. One inch and then another along the loose and crumbling ledge. His arm no longer sensate, his eyes stinging in the wind, his opened mouth dry and needles in his lungs, he moved and did not think. Pebbles rattled off the ledge and bounded to a new and distant location on the earth, but he merely moved against wind and mountain, time and probability.

Many hands reached when he was still far too far away. They clutched and whispers said, "Just an-

浪
人

other step! Softly! Just an inch!" Then he was wrenched onto the open space and drowned in talking faces. It took two men to pry his fingers from the young man's arm, then he sat an endless little time battling with the altitude. They waited.

Then he began to curse them with every foul and angry word that he could marshal to his tongue. The substance of it was, "What kind of dog-brained fools are you to travel so sure a way to death!" When he had done, a young woman said without rancor, "There is no other way for us." He listened then and heard the price of sailing in the cheapest boat to the city on the other side of the Mountain. He looked hard from face to face when told many came this way knowing some must die. A voice said, "Look!" A finger pointed and he saw another party coming up this way.

There was only one thing to do. He went down to the village and worked, earned length after length of rope and brought it to the Precipice. Securing one end here, he edged to the far side against the indignation of the wind. Tied firmly there, it now became a minute gesture to ward off fear and perhaps even a death or two. He squinted and rooted in the past for a pulley on which to haul their goods. Without the load, even more might reach the other side.

In the meantime, he carried the babies and the old, and brought the others in tiny herds at which he yelled and cursed and tyrannized until each was brought across alive. When they thanked him and felt for coins, he said, "The last party paid too much. Let's say they paid for you, huh?"

They nodded and shrugged and went on their ways in the great discomfort of a gift as big as life. The Mountain, cheated of its daily toll, waited in silence.

One day he had the great good fortune to fall ill and lie listlessly in his bed of straw while a very lucky man slipped off the cliffs into the mists below. The sick man groaned because he'd not been there, and began to think of the eventual time he'd not return and the Mountain would claim its own again without another interruption.

The only solution lay in finding another man to replace him, and that man finding another to replace *him* in an infinity to match the Mountain's. But how could this be done? The torch is not lightly handed down and one failure is the end of all succession. He turned and turned upon his bed searching for a way to do battle with the Mountain after he had gone.

When the answer came, he rejected it and thought again. When it returned, he tilted his head and studied it. He said, "Very, very hard, the hardest thing a man could do. And very long." His eyes warmed. Those words recommended it; by them, he knew it was the answer. The illness fell from him like rags.

He rose, went to the iron smith and bargained

浪
人
137

for a pick. He climbed up to the ledge, surveyed the Enemy and, as the wind rose to a tempest, drove the pick into the rocky mountainside with all his strength and hate and love and yearning. The Mountain seemed to groan, then it flung back chips into his face. They cut deep. He squinted looking for the place the pick had struck. He struck again and the handle broke.

He stepped back and shouted to the peak: "I'm coming in there after you! Right through your gut and out the other side!" There was thunder; there was rain, but he shook his fist and laughed: "Fight back with all you have and you're still a fallen foe! You're finished, done, you're through!"

Then he laid his cheek against the cold, wet rock and said, "You didn't mean to kill. You're just a mountain that happened to be here." Then he stood back and shouted, "But *I'm* here now!" and went on down for another pick.

One more holy showman. . . .

There was a small rattle of pebbles into the abyss. A new handle in his hand, he struck the Mountain and said, *"There!"* for every tear that had been shed before this hungry peak. He struck a thousand times for each body that had writhed through space.

But anger has its drawbacks. Gritting his teeth all day only made them hurt. So he sent as much of his fury as he could spare back down to the village and worked alone. He worked simply because there was work to do. It seems this kind is best.

And slowly a tiny navel appeared in the great stone belly, and the echoes of rattling rock were carried on every wind.

A hand touched his shoulder. He turned and was shocked to see a very old woman behind him with a covered bowl of rice. She had crawled up all this way to give him a luxury that she herself enjoyed hardly once a year.

Shame crushed him and he stared at the outline of his folly. He'd put on the same spectacle that all saints stage, whether they will or not. A show of selflessness sure to bore everyone for all time to come.

He growled: "Mother, sit. My hunger for this rice will not be satisfied until you eat every single grain of it. Now, sit and rest yourself and eat."

But even as he said it, he guessed he really *had* the holy habit, a winged and haloed monkey on his back.

The little woman put down the rice, straightened and reached up high to cuff his ears. It hurt.

"I didn't crawl all the way up this miserable path

to be treated rudely by a boor—and surely not to eat my own small gift! If this were *my* meal, I'd much prefer to have it comfortably at home. Why must you make me *earn* it by climbing for an hour in the wind and cold? What ever happened to respect for older folk? Are the young so wise so soon? Now, you will sit and you will eat. What's more, you'll do it now. I can't go until you've finished because I need the bowl."

He ate. It tasted no better than millet.

Taking her pilgrimage as a warning, he decided to end this sort of thing before it got under way and made one more shrine in a shrine-packed land. Yes, he, too, had almost missed the point of the whole affair—which was simply that at last he'd found congenial work. And when it ceased to be work, he'd have to start all over in that miserable job-hunting of the spiritually unemployed. No, he liked his Mountain and he meant to keep it like any normal pig.

Henceforth, he took parties across the Precipice by day and sometimes asked a jot of food, or perhaps a pick, a mallet or a spike if they could spare it. Only at night did he dig.

And the light of his fire—like that of any vulgar saint—flickered like a lower star to the people of the Plain.

His shadow dancing on the rock, he smashed tool after tool to splinters against the angry Mountain. But he dug without anger, thought or aspiration.

He was himself the pick and mallet, he was the rock, he was the wind and the fire and the Mountain.

He swung and struck and swung and struck. And just before too great fatigue, he lay by the wind-whipped fire, thanked all aches so that they could go and slept profoundly for an hour, seldom more. Then he rose to swing and strike and swing and strike on down through the hours of the night.

And each morning the ashes of last night's fire were a few inches farther inside the Mountain.

Nor did he know when Tranquillity came at last. The Groundhog of Paradise, it fears its shadow and surely will not stay when looked upon.

Monster's heir. . . .

When still many villages away, the young swordsman heard of the Tunnel. He was interested but did not relate it to his goal. He heard the digger called a saint and recognized the need of league-leaping mutants to inspire men to shuffle forward some minor fraction of an inch. And, as he went his own leagues, he wondered wryly that his Devil and that 浪

人

Saint shared between them this same village that he sought.

Only looking at the distant mountain from the village street did he guess the two were one. But he did not cry out at being victim of a joke. To him, sainthood was a villain's loophole of escape. And that was that, for the Time of Thought was past.

He bought new clogs, packed food and walked around the Mountain. It took three weeks and something of a day. In the circuit, he studied the Mountain's height and the stubborn diameter of stone. He studied weather and the way that age comes to the arms, the back and mind. He studied penance and the heart of a man he no longer knew.

Then he sat in the cold wind calculating. He converted tears to numbers, made ambition linear, multiplied the decimals of age and ill, and divided all by the sum of joy.

Coming to a figure, he rose, returned to the village and took the Highway home.

The Return was a great event. The Great Daimyo could not refrain from touching him and asked his needs as any servant would. The young swordsman gave thanks gravely but spoke no word of that which the Palace was most keen to know.

At last they were alone. The Uncle asked with all the quietness he knew, "And now—you are at peace?"

The young man looked at him with the cool beauty of the wind: "I have one more journey."

The Uncle let a moment pass then murmured, "When?"

"In ten years I must go again. Then I'll be at peace."

The older man leaned forward and stared a little stupidly: "Ten *years?*"

The young man laid his sword upon the *tokonoma* rack and said, "Nor will I touch this while I wait. I've studied to equal his excellence. Now I must try to match his coming rustiness and age."

The Uncle felt a sort of panic as if he were cage to a wild bird: "But why ten years instead of five or nine?"

Not concerned with being understood, the young swordsman answered to the distant hills: "In ten years, the Tunnel will be almost done. I'll cut off his hands, an inch before he's through."

The Uncle, who understood quite well, looked at this serenely handsome face and felt a chill of fear. He'd never known such a calm, cool wish to kill— except in a ronin who had destroyed his brother's house.

Another young man dies. . . .

The young swordsman rebuked his Uncle for dying and himself became the Great Daimyo of universal choice. Conscientious in wars and revenue, and justice not yet formulae in books, his years paraded past with wives and concubines, sons and lovers whom he did not know, and he developed all the martial skills save one.

Hearing that his teacher on the mountain-top had only days to live, the young Daimyo climbed the path alone and sat beside his bed upon the mat. There were no words exchanged. And when the Moment came, both looked away as if content to be rid of one another.

Yet, going down the path, the young Daimyo heard a pine cone fall and whirled to face the sound. Seeing that fear had returned, he began to practice *kendo* in his mind. He spent hours fencing as he sat in moveless meditation, hours in practice as he slept, and the untouched sword upon the *tokonoma* rack never left his hands by night or day.

The tenth year was something of a torment. With immense effort, he lived each hour of each separate day, fought the doubt of his calculations on how fast a man can dig and struck away the lyric wish to run swiftly down the road and meet the Man and have it done. Instead he stayed at the loom of state and wove his wars, his revenue and justice, too, and made sons somewhat mechanically. Nor did he once look into the *tokonoma* where the Sword hung in wooden space.

Upon the last day of the tenth year, he appointed a surprised regent, drew the sword and scabbard out of its cloth cover, picked up a pound or two of oval golden coins, the Ronin's sword and a basket hat that covered face and head, and strode through the Gate onto the Road.

A day too late, he was surprised to find he'd left his comb behind. The people of his Palace looked on it and were still, for such a happening is fraught with significance. A lost comb indicates that the vanished owner has become another person.

His calculation in cold wind could not anticipate the Mountain's heart. It was of rock beyond the hardness of all rock that must be chipped away in slivers and in grains. So it was that the young Daimyo walked into the village a good two years ahead of the schedule that he'd set.

By now, it was the Village of the Digging Saint and there were sweepstakes on the day that he'd be through. There was such prosperity that no one

浪
人

thought beyond that day. Pilgrims came in hordes, and paid inflated prices to eat and sleep and take home souvenirs. Splinters of the Saint's discarded tools ran high and threads of his rags were immured in little golden charms. There was a rich and thriving merchant class that bore up well under the despising of the poorer nobles of the fief. Though taxes rose, of course, there were few who did not dine on rice each day. Millet was the gloomy past and the future was endless, for the Mountain was too great to really let a tunnel through.

The young Daimyo took the wing of an inn distant from the town and sat out the day in most intriguing seclusion. Knowing that "to wait" is a frame of mind and that no time actually can be wasted, he occupied himself with meditation under the sun and practice with the sword in the midnight courtyard. On no more evidence than this, word went out that he'd come on some romantic vendetta and that he planned refined revenge on a villain yet unknown. It made exciting whispered conversation. And, of all the speculation on who the villain was, none guessed it was the Saint, the financial mainstay of the fief.

But one can maintain a frame of mind and refuse to waste one's time for just so long. It was easier to wait ten years and a hundred miles away. Here, looking at the Mountain, meditation became a quiet riot and his hind parts went to sleep. He went outside and listened to the talk. Chatter guessed the

Tunnel's consummation would come within fifteen minutes or as many years. In a village where none had so much as shaken a fist at the Mountain, authorities on excavation multiplied like flies. He strolled away then began to walk.

He understood the Enemy worked at night. This meant he slept by day. So without another thought, the young Daimyo climbed the mountain path to find out for himself.

The wind was sharp and cold. It whipped his clothes as if to press him back. Along the path was a large delta where diggings had been dumped and there the black eye of the opening. He stepped inside. The air was warm as an embrace. Holding out his hand, he went forward in the balmy midnight with the caution of one who expects a wall at any step. He counted up to ten and ten again and many tens. His arm grew tired. Unwillingly, he raised his sword arm and felt the darkness as he walked. The tens became confused and soon he could only gauge the length by his own astonishment.

The young Daimyo walked into the sweat-hot heart of the Mountain until the entrance was a dot behind and still his hand could feel no end.

Nor could he feel above nor either of the sides. The Tunnel began to frighten him for there was grandeur here that should not be. One man dug this alone? And that man was the Beast? Oh, how heavily his crimes must weigh upon his sleepless

浪
人

nights! Far from Goodness, this was a monument to Sin and all these pilgrims mistook blood for benefaction. They could never have entered here, knowing the reason for the Work!

He never reached the end. There were echoes that jelled into voices, and a torch behind him. Behind the bobbing dot of light, they admired and exclaimed. They saw him and were hushed, then began whispering in awe as in a shrine. Someone asked when it would be finished and the man with the torch grunted. The young Daimyo said, "If it's ever finished." They looked at him and he said, "What a pity if something stopped the Digging Saint just inches from the end!" The man with the torch laughed, "Why then the villagers would finish it!" and the young Daimyo persisted: "But to get so far and not live to see it through!"

Then, to his horror, the man with the torch laughed again and said, "Oh, I'll finish it, all right!"

The young Daimyo turned sharply. For the first time since his childhood he faced the Enemy.

The man was even larger than he'd remembered. Under his rags and the touch of gray, his giant body was lean, and hard as the rock that it did battle with. He presented a picture of virile power that was absurd in a penitent and ridiculous in a saint.

The young Daimyo's eyes moved over this magnificence as if looking for some alleviating flaw, and he blushed in the darkness with admiration he could not escape. Then he saw those laughing eyes move over him and the big man murmured, "So much alike that you're her ghost," as if they had no audience.

Instantly, the young man's hand went to his sword: "I've waited since the Fight at the Landing to avenge her." The pilgrims backed away in gasping shuffles, but not so far they'd miss details. The big man turned to follow then said amiably over his shoulder, "Kill me when I'm finished, hah?" and the young Daimyo answered, "What's to stop me now?"

The big man stopped and turned. The friend-liness in his face made the young man rage.

"You haven't lived a *gishi* to make your first duel only a kind of extermination. As a just man, you'll let me fight when I'm ready. And I intend to see the light come bursting through that wall."

"I'll not let you have that satisfaction!"

"Oh? Then hack at my back as I turn away."

Having thought only the just acted with justice, the young man grated with fury: "You don't even die right! Oh, now I really hate you!"

The big man smiled: "You have her passion, too, and the conviction that it makes you grand."

"And what's so grand about this passion that makes you dig! It's a long, drawn-out whimper for salvation like a dog out in the rain!"

Again the laugh and echoes and the sound of restive pilgrims: "Yes, that's it! I want to be saved! But not from Hell. From wakefulness! This Tunnel

浪
人
149

earns me sleep. And it comes in little bits and snatches that last about as long as we have talked. *There's* Salvation, boy!"

"And the day you've finished, you'll never sleep again."

The big man looked at him and said, "Yes, I know. I've often thought of that." He smiled. "But now you're here with passion and with steel to answer all that for me. My thanks. Death's easy. Anyone can die that has to. And I promise to make you work to do this favor for me. You haven't dedicated your entire life to a beast like me, to have the climax easy, have you, huh?"

The young man said, "Yes, you work," and strode through the parting crowd. There was silence behind him. He had a desperate wish to look back but didn't.

Then the big voice came undulating to him from an echoing distance: "Boy? And what of *you* when this is done? *Hah?*"

He stopped and swallowed the jagged fact that he'd looked no further past that day than had the prospering villagers.

A black lacquer box....

A man always smiles a little sadly when he learns something with his heart, as if the loss of youth were not the gain of age. The young Daimyo smiled very sadly as he dropped a picture from his mind. In it, the Beast cried out and cowered as he, the Hero, revealed himself and his intent. Now, he saw it as a childish scene, and impossible with the fearless adversary whom he needed to make his triumph great.

And he'd have it no other way. To become Legend, the battle must be close, a match of might and the victory uncertain. Then that one last brilliant burst that would leave him standing weary and alone, and the noble enemy admiring him through streams of blood as he lay dying on the ground. A strict design to give the proper thrill to all the infant samurai of time to come, to those who'd never touch a sword and those who had, and those who had and felt *Bushido's* image should be improved 浪 upon. And so the Necessary Lie makes all legends 人 come to sound alike.

The Village was no longer there when he returned. It was now a hostile camp and anger stared at him from every eye. No longer the nice, quiet gentleman who sat in meditation all day long, he was Evil and the Beast come to snatch away their Saint, Prosperity and Rice, and the very village name.

As he went into the courtyard, a rock bounced off the wall ahead. Others fell about him, small rocks and never close because his sword was long.

The days that followed were formicate with peasant spite. They dragged their feet, brought food that was not quite hot, answered sullenly, spilled things and forgot commissions. All the minutiae that, noticed, require ceaseless reprimand or ignored, increase.

Impatient in the atmosphere of unofficial war fought with weapons he disdained, the young Daimyo one evening took the path up the mountain in the wind. He entered the Tunnel and walked toward the dot of light and pounding at the other end. The echoes bounded like a game of iron battledore and shuttlecock.

The big man worked naked to spare his rags. His body glistened with exertion and the Mountain's heat. The young Daimyo said loudly, "Still digging up your dead?" and the giant in wet jewels turned and smiled and said, "You've come to keep me company!"

The young man watched with relish and in a

pause said, "Have you thought that every blow brings you just a moment nearer death?" The big man laughed: "Yes, all of us and even you!" His body knotted as he struck the spike and his great balls swung like clappers of a bell.

The young man laughed, struck his thighs and said, "That's it! Strike hard!" Then quietly: "But you're different from all of us. You know the date and moment of your death. Doesn't that take a little sweetness from your penitence?"

The big man turned and palmed sweat off his chest and gut: "This isn't penitence. No tunnel as long as time itself nor the forgiveness of all the gods could bring to life the men I've killed or ease the pain I've caused. No, not penitence. Only a fool clings to his sins and pets them like a cat."

For some reason at just that moment, the young man remembered his teacher remarking that shame is the soil of all virtue, good manners and good morals. He flung the idea from him and leaned forward to exclaim, "Oh, then you've forgiven yourself! How nice. Then just what *is* this hole you dig?"

"A tunnel, just a tunnel."

"And what are you? Still a beast or now a saint?"

"A digger, just a digger."

The young man laughed: "And soon a corpse, just a corpse."

The big man laughed with him and returned to striking rock from rock. Suddenly exasperated, the

浪
人

young Daimyo strode down the Tunnel and out into the winds of ice.

He took to coming in to sit and watch through the early hours of the night. And at the entrance always yelled, "Still digging up your dead?" and the big man yelled, "Come in!" Sometimes he sat, sometimes he paced, but always flung barbs into the glistening back. They never seemed to stick.

One night he brought a load of wood: "This is to hurry up the Work. I'll feed the fire so you needn't rest so much." The big man thanked him and struck the rock with all his might.

With a great earth-sigh, a boulder slid down and thudded to the center of the floor. The big man pushed it until the veins knotted at his temples. Not a tremor passed from his great body into the rock. The younger laughed and urged him on, but the boulder would not budge. At last, the big man stopped and took his pick and started tapping it to smaller size. The younger bounded up alarmed: "Are you insane? It will take weeks to break that up!" And he tied his sleeves up to his shoulders and stood beside the other man to push. Four hands made it start to turn. By dawn they'd gone many of the thousand feet ahead. Three nights later, they stood panting in the wind and heard the rock go bounding wildly in the mists below.

The big man gave the younger's back a pat, said, "Thanks," and walked inside. The other went down the path without a word.

The next night, he brought the wood and fed the fire, then laid aside his fine new clothes. He'd brought a new mallet and a spike. He placed the spike and just before the first blow said, "I'll do anything I can to haste you to your grave." The big man smiled and the blow rang out.

"And in case you do not understand, see that black lacquer box I brought tonight? That's to carry home your head."

The big man smiled: "Then let's hurry, huh? I don't want to keep you from all the other things you have to do. Because of me, you've not yet *begun* your life! So hit hard and fast!"

And the Tunnel filled with the noise of doubled work.

And become what I am. .

Every evening of the next two years, the young Daimyo entered the Tunnel with a bundle of wood, 浪
built the fire, laid aside his clothes and greeted the 人
Enemy with the six syllables of hate: "Still digging

up your dead?" Then the two worked steadily through the night.

There was talk at first, then only some. Then none. Very little can be said with words.

It was the fourth month of the thirteenth year with Spring still timid on the slopes. The big man looked over at his young executioner and said, "Tomorrow morning at the Hour of the Ram."

"Tomorrow morning *what*?"

"It will be done."

"Maybe. There *has* been a change in the sound of the rock."

"The Hour of the Ram."

"All right, all right, the Hour of the Ram."

They continued to dig, stopped for tea and rice as they always did, rested as long and rose to work toward dawn neither faster nor slower than before.

In the darkest hours of the night with only the fire crackling obbligato to his pick, the big man stopped. He wondered how long he'd been working alone and looked behind him.

The younger man was standing beyond the fire facing the darkness; his strong back glimmered in the light. He seemed to be wracked with fits of quiet shuddering as if in chill. Then he turned and his face was wet, and he began feeling the big man's body with his eyes, every part of it in a long, selfless study that ended with a cry to the jagged, rocky heavens: *"How terrible to destroy another man!"*

Then he looked into the other's eyes and said

angrily, "How could you destroy when you were made to build! How could you force another man —to soil his hands with your blood in vengeance for all your crimes!"

The big man looked at him: "I'm not forcing you to do anything." The young Daimyo burst out, "But you know I must! You know I will!"

The big man went to him, took him in his arms and laid his cheek upon the young head. He spoke soothingly: "I know and I'm glad you can't forgive. It becomes you and gives meaning to your dream of goodness."

The young man pulled away: "Damn you, don't say this holy trash! You can't woo me from my Vow!"

"I wouldn't want to."

"Trash, trash, all holy trash! Even a saint doesn't want to die!"

"No? Then let me tell you something that you'll never understand. Even before I met them, your Father was a fool and your Mother a slut."

The young Daimyo stared up at him moment after moment. At last he walked away, picked up his mallet and his spike, and they worked wordless through the night.

Midway in the Hour of the Ram, the big man's pick made a sound it had never made before and sank up to the handle with shocking ease. He pulled it slowly out like a spent erection from a womb. Simultaneously there was a spike of hard, pale light

浪
人

thrust in at him and a whirring of cold air that raped the warm and musky dark.

They stood and looked at it, and felt the cold.

Then in sudden frenzy, they attacked the dot of sky and ripped it wide and stretched it big enough to make a window on the world. They pressed forward and leaned out as if there were some special scene to see that had not been seen before. They saw, of course, no view but Destination.

Then both looked down. The Tunnel ended in the face of a cliff higher, steeper, wider and more deadly than its mild brother at the other end. They stared.

The big man pulled back and pressed against the wall. He murmured as if stunned: *"But I was so sure of my direction!"*

The other whispered, "It will take again as long to make a path down there."

The big man said, "Oh, no."

The young man looked at him: "But we must, We can't stop here."

The Ronin walked to the fire: "No, let's have the duel and get it over."

The young voice was loud with anger: "I can't finish this alone! It's not *my* work!"

"It's anyone's. Let them," and he began to walk away. "Bring the swords and let's get out of here. It might cave in."

The young Daimyo didn't move: "But you can't

just leave it like this! Come back here and I'll help. Time's cheap."

The big figure was striding naked toward the other light: "Not mine! No more! Not me!"

The young man screamed after him: "But you can't leave a thing like this undone! It's wrong not to finish what you start!"

And the big voice echoed from a vast distance in the dark, *"The hell with it!"*

—THE END—

浪
人